FOOTBALL IN LONG BEACH

FOOTBALL IN LONG BEACH

MIKE GUARDABASCIO

THE History PRESS

Published by The History Press
Charleston, SC 29403
www.historypress.net

First published 2012

Manufactured in the United States

ISBN 978.1.60949.545.9

Library of Congress CIP data applied for.

For Shar, as always.

CONTENTS

Acknowledgements

When you put time and energy into a project like this and find it mirrored and doubled by so many friends and like-minded historians, the acknowledgements could easily outpace the rest of the book. First, a heartfelt apology to everyone who's been left out—the author is forgetful, not vindictive.

First and foremost, editor Jerry Roberts and the rest of the team at The History Press were fantastic. Jerry was very patient with me when deadlines needed to be flexible and gave me time to do this book right.

Over two dozen people agreed to sit down and be interviewed for this book, and I'm incredibly grateful to have had the chance to speak with them. I was able to talk to every championship coach the city has seen after 1949, and the coach of every Poly CIF champion since Orian Landreth's 1930s teams. Thanks to (in no particular order) Dave Levy, Dick DeHaven, Bill Brady, Dave Radford, Don Norford, Don Wallace, Jeff Turley, Jerry Jaso, Jim McCormick, Jim Stangeland, Joe Carlson, Chris Lewis, Chris Kinder, Gene Noji, Raul Lara, Kirk Diego, Shawn Ashley, Terri Spier, Rob Shock, George Daily-Lyles, Jeff Severson, Bob Keisser, Jim Barnett, Dee Andrews, Mike Giers, Marcedes Lewis, Darnell Bing and Larry Reisbig. Your generosity with your time is greatly appreciated, as is the generosity of the dozens of additional athletes and coaches I've interviewed during my time as a sportswriter.

Thanks also to the chroniclers of this city's history throughout the decades. There isn't room to thank by name all the newspaper and yearbook writers and editors who helped inform my knowledge, but the quality and consistency of the work was shocking.

Individuals at every school were phenomenal. First and foremost, the staff at Poly, from top to bottom, has my gratitude. Principals Joe Carlson and Victor Jarels were very patient with me essentially living on their campus for two months, and Matt Peyton, the school's newspaper advisor, let me use his back room as a private office, even while he was stressing over the impending birth of his son Jacob. The school's librarian, Pamela Oehlman, has my thanks, as do English teachers Judy Haenn, Laura Leaney and Rob Pigott for saying nice things about me ten years ago.

The great Sam Dimas passed away literally hours before I had planned on visiting and interviewing him formally, a loss of knowledge that this book and this city won't fully recover from. The extensive Poly chapter of this volume is dedicated to the memory of Slammin' Sammy.

At Long Beach State, sports information director Todd Miles and his staff were fantastic as always, and I appreciate Todd and athletic director Vic Cegles for letting me rummage through their vast media archives. Dedan Brozino allowed me to camp out in his office for a time while researching. Chris Ruiz, Long Beach City College's sports information specialist, also has my thanks, as does Dr. Ginny Baxter of the LBCC Foundation, who made space for me and my many stacks of yearbooks.

At St. Anthony, athletic director Brian Walsh not only loaned me one of every yearbook in the history of the school but also helped me carry them to my car. Principal Sandy Blazer at Wilson was very helpful; unfortunately, at that school, too, another legend passed away just before a planned interview. The chapter on the Bruins is dedicated to the memory of Skip Rowland.

At the California Interscholastic Federation's Southern Section (CIF-SS) office, historian John Dahlem shared his expertise and allowed me access to their archives, as well as ran off a few hundred pages of very helpful copies. Commissioner Rob Wigod, a proud Long Beach guy, offered a few words of encouragement, as did director of communications Thom Simmons. Thanks to the Long Beach Century Club for giving me hope for the future and a link to our past. The Long Beach Public Library and its librarians and the Long Beach Historical Society and its historians were also helpful.

Long Beach sportswriting legends Jim McCormick and Bob Keisser were both very generous in offering their congratulations and advice. Thanks for that, and thanks to Bob for allowing me access to his records, as well as the *Press-Telegram*'s photo archive.

The helpfulness of the above people would have been futile were it not for the generosity of JJ Fiddler, and Tyler Hendrickson, my fellow sportswriters at the *Gazettes* in Long Beach. They assisted with research and picked up the slack at the newspaper when I was unavailable, without question or complaint. Thanks also to my boss, Simon Grieve, for the opportunity to cover the next chapters of Long Beach sports history while also making a living, and to my editor, Harry Saltzgaver, for making me look like a professional.

Nothing in my career would have been possible without my Popop and Grandma, who each gave me confidence; my dad, who gave me my first notebook; or my mom, who gave me everything else. My eternal gratitude to Paul and Judy Belknap, who awarded me the Jessica Belknap Memorial Scholarship in their daughter's name. Thanks also to my best friend Ryan Thies, his wife Stacy and their son James, who provided me with several much-needed breaks.

A special thanks to my favorite Poly football player of all time, my younger brother, Matt Guardabascio, whose final varsity stat line reads: one false start and one assisted tackle. He was, however, the first student announcer for the team in the modern era, and he transcribed most of the interviews conducted for this book.

Last, and the opposite of least, thanks to my wife, Shar. Despite being a full-time teacher for the first time in her life while I was writing this book, she took the time to make my life easier and to make this book possible, constructing its index, among other chores. I am honored to dedicate this book to her and to the city of Long Beach, our shared love.

Introduction

For the last 125 years, football in Long Beach has been less of an interest and more of a preoccupation. The city incorporated on February 10, 1888, declaring itself as an official member of a burgeoning Southern California landscape. Just a few months later, the Long Beach Foot Ball Club traveled north on the Southern Pacific to play the Alliance Athletic Club of Los Angeles in what the *Long Beach Journal* referred to as "a match game of foot ball." On April 29, 1888, that group of Long Beach athletes took part in the first football game ever played in Southern California.

A few years later, the citizens of Long Beach dissolved its city status, and it didn't incorporate permanently until 1897. In the intervening years, however, its citizens did not stop playing football. Incorporating into a city was a tricky proposition, but football was a necessity and has remained one for over a hundred years. In a city where murals fade, budgets are slashed and iconic stores are shuttered, football is a tradition that remains undiminished.

Poly and Wilson, the city's two oldest high schools, have been meeting in "The Big Game" since 1932, thirty-four years before the first NFL Super Bowl was played. Poly has famously produced more NFL athletes than any other high school in the nation (the competition isn't even close).

To trace a history of football in Long Beach is to walk the roads of the history of football itself. After all, the first forward pass predates the first Poly team (fielded in 1908) by only two years. The Jackrabbits actually predate the first NFL game by twelve years. The Pittsburgh Steelers are one of America's most storied pro football franchises but, by the time they played their first contest in 1933, Long Beach already had five schools competing (Poly, Wilson, St. Anthony, Long Beach City College and Jordan).

On the collegiate level, Long Beach State has a fascinating, complex past that culminated in the death of George Allen, the NFL coaching legend who brought a maelstrom of national attention to a struggling, small-time program. His death, long rumored to be the result of pneumonia caught from a celebratory Gatorade bath following his final game as coach of the 49ers, effectively killed the team, too. The Vikings of LBCC, a program still going strong, have won five national championships.

Long Beach's history, viewed through the lens of its favorite sport, is a story of natural disasters, racial integration, authoritarian injustice and, above all, a story of triumph and a tradition that has burned brightly throughout the decades.

You hold in your hand a guidebook, a labor of love in the service of that tradition. It is my hope that this book will help further and broaden the city's appreciation of its proud history and spread the word. The first half of the book is dedicated to Poly, a school that contains well over that portion of Long Beach's accomplishments and championships, but recognition is owed to all of the city's high schools and colleges who have together woven a remarkable story. It's a story that could easily fill a book four times the size of the one you hold in your hands, were there room. The great thing about a history as proud as Long Beach's, of course, is that it never stops being told or argued about in the stands (or bookstores).

So when the drumline starts, when the halide and sodium floodlights are popping on all over the city this fall, as they do every fall, when the chilly autumn winds start blowing over the artificial turf at Vets, keep this book close. You never know when you might see the next chapter being written on the field right in front of you.

CHAPTER ONE

LONG BEACH POLY

Home of Scholars, Champions and More Champions

In 1895, Long Beach High School opened its doors at its first location on Third Street and Locust Avenue. One title change, two changes of address, a complete rebuilding and 117 years later, Long Beach Poly has firmly established its reputation as one of the best high schools in America. The school's football team has won eighteen California Interscholastic Federation (CIF) Southern Section championships, more than any other in history, and has produced over sixty NFL athletes, more than any other in the nation.

As to how that happened, you'll get as many answers as you have time to hear. Some say it's the soil, since the team didn't start winning championships until the campus was moved to its current location at 1600 Atlantic Avenue. Some (like Poly alum and former NFL director of football operations Gene Washington) have suggested it's the uniforms. But there's no doubt that the school has had the finest string of football athletes and coaches that a high school could ever ask for, stretched over a nearly incomprehensible time period in the day-by-day world of prep sports.

Sports Illustrated, *USA Today* and ESPN have all recognized Poly as (historically) having the country's best high school football program. *Sports Illustrated* named Poly the country's best sports high school; *Sporting News* called it "a football trade school."

It's a history so rich that it's been retold countless times. The first published attempt at a comprehensive history was an exhaustive four-part account written by Ray Fulwiler for the *Long Beach Press* that ran in 1924. The next year, the paper put together its first "All-Time" Poly team, an exercise that has remained popular over the last eight decades, even as the school's earliest stars have faded out of memory and into legend.

Here, you will find the most complete account of Poly's football history ever printed—and, even here, over a dozen Jackrabbits who have made appearances in the NFL are passed over, proving that, as the Poly student body has sung for decades, perhaps it really is hard to be a Rabbit.

THE EARLY DAYS, 1895–1915

A long time ago, back before the memory of any living Poly fans (no matter what they tell you), Long Beach High School wore red and white as its colors, and the school couldn't care less about the sport it is now most identified with. The color change happened in 1898, when a pro baseball team donated its old green and gold jerseys to the school. Around that same time, the school adopted the Jackrabbit as its mascot because the athletic field on campus was hopping with them.

In the 1907–08 school year, the school offered five sports: tennis, track, handball, basketball and baseball. Long Beach High School's heart wasn't on the playing field but behind the podium: the school had a well-known debate team that was difficult to beat, both in oratorical skill and in student body support. As a 1907 yearbook put it, "Debating has served to create school spirit more than any other activity. Long Beach High School closes the season with an enviable record, not only because of victories won, but because of the great interest which has been put into this phase of school life." The writers of that passage had no idea what a whirlwind was to hit the campus the next fall, when the Jackrabbits fielded their first football team to compete in the autumn of 1908, the first date in a century-long love affair with the sport.

By all accounts, the Jackrabbits owe a great debt to a lanky student named Fred Trude, the scarecrow-like first baseman for the school's baseball team. After a few years of students talking about organizing a football team, "Gov" Trude decided to just go ahead and do it. In the fall of 1908, Long Beach High School fielded a team of fifteen young men, all clad in borrowed rugby uniforms. Trude put the call out, made the team's first schedule and handled all the administrative duties for the city's inaugural prep campaign.

Ad for the debate team, the first love of Poly students at the turn of the century. *Poly yearbook.*

On October 17, the Jackrabbits played their first game, a 16–0 loss to Pasadena High, the school that would serve as one of their fiercest rivals for the next several years. Two weeks later, they played Occidental Prep and won their first game, 10–0. Despite the low numbers, a lack of administrative support and a team of players who also served as their own coaches, the Jackrabbits went 5–3 that first year, with one of the three losses coming to USC's freshmen, who beat the Long Beach trailblazers 22–6.

If you're looking for evidence of how different the world was in 1908, look no further than the team's first quarterback, Stub Smith. Smith starred for the first few weeks of the season but ultimately quit the team, having withdrawn from high school in order to marry Miss Eloise Starling of Kansas City a month and a half after playing his first high school football game. Floyd Frazier, the first in a long line of fleet-footed Poly players, took over for Smith.

A 1909 yearbook proclaims "The pigskin is a part of Long Beach High now. Football has come to stay. For three years we have tried to make football an interest, and now we know we have succeeded. There can be no doubt that from now on, football will be the game of the High School." Indeed, by the next year, things were already looking up, at least in terms of support. Poly had a coach, for starters, as Roy Coffin was the first to hold the clipboard. Trude stayed on as team manager, assembling the team's schedule again and even managing to find and fund fifteen brand new uniforms, which helped boost the team's numbers. Coffin, as the team's first coach, would implement an idea that has remained a core tenet of the school's philosophy, ordering Trude to put together the hardest schedule he could muster.

But the schedule proved a little too hard for Coffin's Jackrabbits, and he quickly experienced another truth of Jackrabbit life. It's hard to stay the coach for long if you're not winning. The team went 2–4–1, beating Occidental Prep and Hollywood High, but it lost to USC and rival Pasadena Bulldogs again that year. Coffin did not return the next season.

Still, things were coming together at Long Beach High. The yearbook, thanking Trude once again for overcoming transportation issues and wrangling another season together, proclaims, "This has been only the second year of football in our school. Of course it will stay. No one doubts that anymore."

Clarence Russell took over coaching duties for the 1910 and 1911 seasons, bringing with him the school's first league title in his first year. The 1910 team started 4–0, winning its games by a combined 93–0, including a 16–0 win over the Bulldogs. But a 6–6 tie in the league finale meant the title was shared. As there was no organizing body for Southern California high school sports at that point, the league title was the highest championship available to the school. But that didn't stop the already impatient Jackrabbit fans from finding something to complain about. A section in a Long Beach yearbook reads, "May we be able to keep the football championship next year, and keep it without its being 'tied.'"

The school's first title defense, though, fared poorly—a 2–3 effort that proved to be Russell's last year as coach. The next year, a popular physical education teacher named R.D. Elliott took over the reins, remaining the head of the program for four seasons. In 1912, the league title returned to Long Beach with a 6–0 start. But it was once again a shared championship, Long Beach having suffered a season-ending defeat at the hands of Pasadena, 14–9. The Jackrabbits did manage a notable 21–13 defeat of San Diego High, finding a way to win despite San Diego using a new form of offense, what was then termed as "a series of forward passes." The school began another long-held tradition in 1912, as the offensive and defensive lines were universally deemed bigger and stronger than that of opponents.

The next two years saw the Jackrabbits fall from the top as a tie and a close 6–0 loss to rival Santa Ana ended their league title chances both times.

Action shots of Poly in 1912, just three years after its program started. These are among the first action shots ever taken of the Jackrabbits. *Poly yearbook.*

In 1914, they finally got over on the Trojans, defeating the USC frosh team. They also beat the Army-Navy Military Academy. The 1915 squad, Elliott's last as head coach, was big on speed and small on luck, going 2–3–3 in heartbreaking fashion.

In an old-time refrain that would come back to haunt the Jackrabbits, the yearbook praised the "wonderful machine" of the team's defense but bemoaned an utter inability to score. "Many times during the year, with only a few yards to go for a touchdown, they failed to get the necessary 'punch' to send them over the line," reads one passage, describing a situation all-too familiar to some fans. The team only allowed twenty-four points all season but scored just thirty-nine—all of those points coming in two games. It had three consecutive scoreless ties, followed by a pair of 6–0 defeats to rivals Santa Ana and Pasadena. Santa Ana scored its only touchdown on an interception return, prompting Long Beach fans to jeer the other side as "Lucky Ana."

The disappointment of the year aside, the foundation was officially laid. Just eight seasons after Long Beach High School had fielded its football team, it was firmly established as a Southern California power. The school had a handful of league titles, a fan-base that was now bordering on rabid and a pair of decent rivalries. All it needed was the right coach to push it over the top and into national prominence. The next season, the powder keg would find its spark, and nothing would ever be the same.

FIRST CHAMPIONSHIP: EDDIE KIENHOLZ, 1916–1922

Edgar "Eddie" Kienholz's arrival on the football field of what was now known as Long Beach Poly marked a new beginning for both him and the school. Kienholz's first year saw a team that returned almost no players with any experience, size or talent. Poly didn't win a single game in the Los Angeles County League in 1916 and was drubbed by Pasadena and San Diego, the latter defeating the Jackrabbits 62–0. The California Interscholastic Federation started hosting playoff games for the first time that year, giving teams something besides a league championship to play for. But Poly would not participate that season, thanks to its 3–4–1 record.

Kienholz was so close to members of his team that in later years he would request that he not be mentioned as contributing to the *Press-Telegram*'s "All-Time Poly" list, so he didn't offend any players he left off. But in 1916, the task before him must have seemed monumental. He literally had to teach the team how to score. All of its previous practice time had been dedicated to defense, not surprising to anyone who had noticed the team's half-dozen scoreboard doughnuts the previous year. It took a year to right the ship, but after the sour outing in 1916, the Kienholz-era Poly teams would compile a 43–7–1 record.

Each of the next three years would go down as featuring the best team in the school's history. In 1917, the Jackrabbits won the Los Angeles County League championship and posted a 7–1–1 overall record. The team experienced a strange disruption in November, when Kienholz was drafted to fight in World War I. "Our coach was called to the colors at a critical time of the season," reads the yearbook. But Kienholz had trained his men well, and the Jackrabbits were as much a machine as a football team at that point.

Team captain Jim Lawson coached them for three weeks while the school cast around for a temporary replacement. The Jackrabbits won all three games, including a 67–0 defeat of Santa Barbara, the most points the team had scored in its history. They also ran over Pasadena, 28–0. Lawson would be named Poly's first-ever All-American and would go on to be the team's second player to play professionally, suiting up for the short-lived New York Yankees team of the NFL. Lawson was a teammate of Hall of Famer Red

Coach Edgar Kienholz (center, surrounded by assistants, managers and captains) in service uniform, shortly before leaving Poly to fight in World War I. *Poly yearbook.*

Grange's while in New York, playing a few seasons of football on hallowed ground at Yankee Stadium.

Despite the promising 7–0–1 start to the year, the Jackrabbits were ousted from the playoffs in the semifinal, falling 9–0 to Pomona. The next season, Kienholz was still overseas fighting in Germany, his thoughts on Long Beach, where a wife he had only been married to for a few months and a team he had only been coaching for the same soldiered on without him. That season would go down as one of the strangest in Poly's history.

The Jackrabbits, temporarily being coached by assistants George Capron and Cyril Tipton, went 4–1 but were unquestionably the best high school team in the Southland. The influenza epidemic of 1918 prevented them from proving it on the field, however, and, while the Long Beach boys were healthy and fit, they couldn't find enough competition to play. Whether it was the bracing salt in the sea air, or just blind luck, Long Beach and its citizens skated by relatively unscathed—over 500,000 Americans died in the epidemic, but sleepy Long Beach lost only a few handfuls of citizens.

The team opened the season with a 52–0 victory over Whittier, in a game that saw the team "breathe the old Kienholz spirit," according to one newspaper. But its next four games were canceled due to opponents' illness, and the Jackrabbits would play only one more high school all year, defeating Santa Ana 38–0 on Thanksgiving. They also beat Whittier State and an organization of dockworkers called the Keel Club, picking up their only loss of the season to the Naval Reserves of San Pedro.

Roy "Bullet" Baker starred on the 1918 team as the fullback and linebacker (he also played baseball and ran track) before moving on to USC and starting a decade-long pro football career (becoming Poly's first pro player) with the Yankees and, most notably, the Green Bay Packers. (When Baker joined the Packers, the team was just starting its sixth season, and Baker was its seventh starting quarterback.) In 1918, he was named state player of the year almost by default, as influenza-ravaged California provided little competition to Baker or Poly.

The Poly student body was less than sympathetic. The editor of the yearbook that year wrote, "Every high school had refused to give our boys a crack at their fragile organizations, and Long Beach was forced to search for games outside of high school circles." The team did draw acclaim for its fighting spirit against the Naval Reserves, grown men who outweighed the Poly players by at least fifteen pounds a position, and they only lost 21–7. The Jackrabbits, with no challengers for the title of best team in California, declared themselves champions of the CIF since they were the only team willing to play. The CIF, however, canceled the playoffs and smacked down the Poly boasting, setting the stage for an even uglier clash between the two organizations a few years later.

THE GREATEST SEASON? 1919!

The next year, the team had a chip on its shoulder and almost its entire roster back. Baker graduated and went on to USC, but "Jazz" Lawson, running back Phil Tiernan and 1919 team captain and quarterback Chet Dolley were all ready to suit up in the green and gold. Because of the shortened season of 1918, extra years of eligibility were granted to senior players, a rule that benefited Lawson in particular. Perhaps more importantly, Kienholz had returned safely from World War I and was ready to get back to coaching.

The team that Kienholz coached that year is arguably the greatest in the history of the city and perhaps even the greatest high school football team in the history of America. It finished the season with a schedule of all victories, going 12–0 and outscoring its opponents by a combined total of 549–21. That total includes a 1–0 win achieved by forfeit. When the Jackrabbits finished playing, they had won three championships: Poly's first CIF title, the first championship of California and the American Southwest crown.

It was clear from the first game that the team was taking no prisoners, defeating Compton 71–0 in the first game the future league mates ever played against each other. After that, the team beat Whittier 69–0 and Whittier State 56–7. League opponents fared no better, as the Jackrabbits beat Los Angeles Poly, Los Angeles High and took the forfeit from Jefferson in stride. A 59–0 defeat of Coronado and a 41–0 smackdown of rival Pasadena on Thanksgiving rounded out the regular season, as the Jackrabbits and their swelling group of fans rushed eagerly towards the playoffs.

These Jackrabbits were fast starters, scoring a touchdown to take a lead in the first quarter of every game except for one. In the semifinals of the playoffs, they defeated Santa Monica 21–0, in what has to be considered a nail-biter for that season. Then they met Fullerton in their first-ever CIF championship game, a contest with a lot of excitement in the papers beforehand but absolutely none on the field: Poly beat them 47–0 to claim its first CIF title.

After that, the Jackrabbits beat Dinuba in the State semifinals, 41–0, which set up a game with Berkeley High for the state title, the first to be awarded to a California high school team. Here, finally, was some competition, as Berkeley scored 14 of the 21 points that Poly's foes mustered all season. Just under 12,000 fans gathered at Tournament Park for the game. The seemingly invincible Jackrabbits, expected to win by a huge margin, went up 7–0 in the first quarter on a fifty-five-yard touchdown run by Dolley, the quarterback. It looked like they might be headed for another blowout, but Berkeley quickly answered and tied the score. Henry Lefebvre put Poly up by a touchdown at the end of the first quarter, but Berkeley would tie it again, and the teams remained in a deadlock.

With just a few minutes left in the game, Dolley dropped back and heaved a pass for Lawson, who leapt high and pulled in a fingertip catch, then dove across the goal line for the game's winning touchdown, giving Poly a 21–14 victory. The season to this point would already deserve consideration for one of the best in Poly's history—but the school's final game is what makes it hard to argue against it.

Promoters of the time sensed a profitability in high school sports, nearly a century before recruiting websites and several decades before TV contracts were even being dreamed of. One of the easiest things to promote was a rivalry that was exotic—not crosstown, but cross-state. So it was that the juggernaut Phoenix Coyotes headed west by train to play Long Beach Poly in the first-ever American Southwest Championship. The Jackrabbits brought an unmistakable momentum with them into the game; the Coyotes brought a six-year winning streak.

In the days before the game was to be held, Poly's campus field had new bleachers constructed on all sides, making a temporary ten thousand-seat stadium where a small high school field had been just days before. The set-up was elaborate enough that Fox Studios shipped actors "Slim" Summerville and Bobby Dunn down to Long Beach to film a football comedy there before the game was played.

As the school was building its stadium, the press was building its story. The Coyotes attended a high school rally at Poly, where local reporters noted that they were "a husky bunch," with two linemen both heavier and bigger than any of the local Jackrabbits. Coach Kienholz "drilled into every player that the game will be won by a small margin," according to one newspaper report.

On January 10, 1920, at 2:15 p.m., the game ball was dropped from a plane flown by the famous barnstormer (and first Long Beach resident issued a flying license) Earl S. Daughtery. Carl May danced on the wings of the plane, waving to the record-setting crowd of well over 12,000 gathered below. Poly students passed out special editions of the *High Life*, the campus newspaper, which served as game programs. On the cover of one of the local papers, a huge headline screamed "Expect Close Game."

The fans probably did, but they didn't get it. Instead, a few hours later, Poly had beaten the Coyotes so thoroughly that there could be no doubt the Jackrabbits were the finest team in America. They scored a touchdown every four minutes and won by the eye-popping margin of 102–0. The game, which immediately passed into legend as "The Big 102," was a brutal and unrelenting assertion of dominance. Tiernan scored 5 of Poly's 15 touchdowns, gaining 333 yards and kicking a dozen extra points, while Lefebvre gained another 205 and scored 4 times. The next day, the newspaper cracked, "Phoenix were lucky to escape with zero." Harry J. Moore recalled later in a *Press-Telegram* history piece that some local merchants were offering hats, shirts and ties to anyone scoring touchdowns. After putting the game well out of reach, the generous Tiernan and Lefebvre began to let their linemen take the ball into the end zone, "To get their share of the haberdashery."

Indeed, it may have seemed that Dolley's biggest responsibility as quarterback and team captain was to make sure that everyone got enough free ties to go around, but Kienholz praised him afterward for the job he had done in his five years at Poly, saying, "He's handled the team better than any team I ever saw."

The famous air-dropped ball and the trophy from the 1919 game against Phoenix.
Photo by the author.

Rare action shots from the 1919 game against Phoenix, possibly the most significant win in Long Beach history. *Poly archives.*

Phoenix, on the other hand, had to slink back to its hometown, guilty and embarrassed. "We have no alibi," said Phoenix's team captain in a newspaper write-up of the game. "We're going back to Phoenix and tell the people we were so outclassed that hope of even scoring was abandoned after five minutes."

The Poly Jackrabbits had played a perfect game to end a perfect season and were champions of the Southwest, which included California, Arizona, New Mexico and Texas. The city immediately fell about itself trying to best memorialize its favorite team's accomplishments. The yearbook featured a lengthy retelling of Shakespeare's *Macbeth* with the football team recast as its characters. The city's government held a special meeting to decide what souvenirs should be given to the players as a token of thanks (miniature gold footballs were eventually agreed upon).

The true legacy of the game may be the players who competed for the Jackrabbits. Dolley, Lefebvre and Curt Richards all went on to star at

USC and were on the 1923 Trojan squad that defeated Penn State in the Rose Bowl, the first-ever bowl appearance for either university and the first bowl game held in the new stadium. Lawson was an All-American at Stanford, captaining the school's 1925 Rose Bowl team. Almost every player on the team went on to a D-1 career. Dutch McCallister, one such player, captained the water polo team at Stanford and would play for America in two Olympics.

"The 1919 Long Beach eleven will always be remembered as the bunch that would not accept defeat," reads a 1919–20 yearbook. Not only that, the team wouldn't accept anything less than perfection. For that, it earned its place in the history books.

Were it not for influenza in 1918 and the upcoming intervention of the CIF in 1920 and 1921, Poly would likely have been a four-time champion. With several key starters back from the 1919 juggernaut, 1920 seemed destined for perhaps an even bigger finish than the record-setting campaign of the previous season. Lawson and Lefebvre returned, and Morley Drury, one of the best athletes ever turned out by the school, was already a star in his freshman season.

Poly's first seven games saw the team post a perfect record, outscoring its opponents 438-0. Kienholz's men opened the season with a 113–0 victory over Harvard Military Academy and proceeded to steamroll everyone they met, with a 49–7 victory over the Pomona College freshmen, their closest game of the year. The Jackrabbits averaged 62.6 points per game, the second best in California history according to *Cal Hi Sports Record Book and Almanac*. After beating Los Angeles Poly 55–0 in the first round of the playoffs, Kienholz talked with school officials and came to a decision: the Jackrabbits had already beaten the best the CIF had to offer. Their plan, revealed to the CIF in ambush fashion by Poly vice-principal Harry J. Moore, was to skip the semifinal and final games (having already defeated all potential opponents by upward of fifty points) and play out-of-state teams in a quest to be named national champions.

The CIF was incensed. Making things somewhat awkward was the fact that Moore, while vice-principal at Poly, was also the president of the CIF, a post he served in for thirty-four years. The CIF minutes of December 9, 1920 read: "Resolved: That Long Beach, by its refusal to complete the schedule for the semifinal and final games, has declared its football season closed. In order for the school to be readmitted, it must disband its football team for the present season." Forty-one of the forty-four schools in the CIF voted to ban the Jackrabbits from the organization, a move that Poly found shocking.

A group shot of the 1920 Poly team that was barred from the CIF. *Poly archives.*

Cartoon in the Poly student newspaper, *High Life*, about the CIF's decision to expel Poly. *Courtesy CIF Southern Section.*

The media agreed. According to the *Los Angeles Times*, the Jackrabbits had simply "decided to step outside and schedule some real games."

The Long Beach papers were less polite. "Why would the CIF demand that Long Beach meet in the championship series a team that it had defeated 50–0 in a regular scheduled contest? There is no logic in that," one newspaper stated. The *High Life* student newspaper published a cartoon mocking the CIF, along with an article so inflammatory that the CIF demanded principal David Burcham send the students to a meeting to apologize. "We have been handed the greenest lemon," wrote Poly's student body. "We can never hope to get justice. It's the case where you can lick anyone separately, but not the whole bunch at once."

The Jackrabbits went ahead and kept preparing for their December 17 game against Everett, a school from Washington. Today, intersectional and interstate games are encouraged as fun ways to help grow high school sports. National tournaments are commonplace and even expected at elite schools. But in 1920, the CIF took Poly's decision to prioritize national-level competition as a slap in the face. The organization demanded that Burcham telegram Everett to inform the school that the Jackrabbits were not champions in any way, shape or form; the CIF also demanded that he send the federation a copy of the telegram for good measure. Fullerton High (the team Poly had drubbed in a title game in 1919) piled on, mounting a challenge to Tiernan's eligibility, claiming he was too old.

The distractions did not help with preparation for a Seagulls team that featured a roster full of college-age players, an unfair advantage granted to Everett by Washington's lenient eligibility rules. In front of nearly 20,000 fans, again squeezed onto Poly's campus field, the Seagulls ambushed the besieged Jackrabbits, handing the team its first loss to a high school team since its semifinal loss to Pomona in 1917. Everett won 28–0, thanks largely to the excellent play of its twenty-one-year-old captain, Leslie Sherman. Kienholz, disgusted with the CIF's political play, had his Jackrabbits take their anger out on the basketball court, where he coached Poly to an undefeated CIF championship that year. The next season presented an interesting set of challenges for student manager Lauren Conley, who was in charge of assembling the team's schedule for 1921. How do you make a schedule for a high school football team that is not allowed to play any high schools in your area? The answer was a nine-game schedule full of junior colleges and Division 1 freshman teams.

Although Lawson, Tiernan and the rest of the old guard from the 1919 team had graduated, the 1921 Jackrabbits were certainly good enough to have been CIF champs, had they been allowed by the CIF to compete in that arena. Against college players, they still went 7–2, with their only losses coming to USC and Pomona College. With Morley Drury, a star in his sophomore season, and brothers Al and Don Hill, the Jackrabbits defeated LaVerne College 105–0 and Cal Tech 76–0. But after a 43–0 win over Loyola College to end the season, there was nothing for the team to do but sit and wait for next autumn, when it would be readmitted to the CIF. One newspaper account states, "Those who saw the Long Beach team in action believe it consisted of as good a bunch of pigskin chasers as could be found in Southern California." The year went down as another lost championship opportunity in the annals of Poly history.

The next year, with Drury captaining the team, the Jackrabbits started strong, defeating the Stanford freshman team 49–0 as part of a 5–0 start. But they lost two of their last three games, including the last game of the year to Pasadena, which ended their playoff chances—this time legitimately, not because someone in an office signed a piece of paper. Thus ended the Kienholz era at Poly. There can be no arguing that he left the school, and the team, better than he found them.

Replacing a coaching legend is never an easy task, but Arthur Schuettner was up to the challenge, winning Poly's second CIF title in 1923, the only year he was head coach of the team. Of course, winning a CIF championship isn't the hardest thing in the world with a player of Morley Drury's ability on the team. Despite having only seven returning players, Schuettner was blessed with the versatile Drury, who started games at center, end, wide receiver, quarterback and fullback for the Jackrabbits and was named All-CIF team three times at three different positions. At USC, Drury started at four positions on three championship teams. Drury was famous for helping opponents up off the ground and for playing with a level of sportsmanship that seemed alien to the brutal sport, a style that earned him the nickname "The Noblest Trojan of Them All." In his final game at USC, against the University of Washington at the Coliseum, he intercepted six passes while leading the team in rushing (his single season record stood for forty years). After his final carry, the crowd of 70,000 gave him a five-minute, uninterrupted standing ovation. "Truly, the best athlete ever turned out in the Southland," said one newspaper.

Drury got his chance to play against college competition early, as Poly continued to play the toughest talent, losing its opening two games to Cal and USC before sweeping through the league. Drury was much more

An action shot from Poly's 1923 CIF championship win over Glendale at the Los Angeles Coliseum. *Poly yearbook.*

multifaceted than Schuettner's playbook, which trashed Kienholz's intricate offense in favor of a scheme that used only five plays with very few variations.

Before the playoffs, Poly held a ceremony to dedicate the recently finished permanent stands at the newly christened Burcham Field on its campus, named for Poly's visionary principal from 1907–41. The cornerstone from the first bleachers on the campus was used as the granite block that the dedication plaque was placed on. Even at just fifteen years old, Poly's football team already had a sense of its own history. That postseason, it added to it, defeating Sweetwater in the quarterfinals 27–7 and crushing Santa Maria 39–0 in the semifinals. The Jackrabbits faced Glendale, a team that Kienholz would later coach in games against Poly. A healthy crowd was on hand at the LA Coliseum to watch a game of caveman football, in which Schuettner urged his Jackrabbits into a defensive performance that only allowed nine points. But Poly only won 15–9 because Schuettner's slim offensive playbook ran out of gas—the Jackrabbits did not attempt a single pass in their second CIF championship win.

Herb Welsh took over coaching duties the next year but failed to defend the title. He was not invited to return. The hatred between Long Beach and Pasadena fans had escalated to the extent that Jackrabbit fans were able to take some measure of comfort in a 13–0 win over the Bulldogs, now termed Poly's "ancient rival" by the yearbook. The next year, Russell Sprong took over. In 1927, he was credited with a CIF championship, as the junior varsity team won the lower-level title over Fullerton, which counted towards a school's total at the time (those levels had a full playoff system in place). In his final three years, Sprong lost all three games against the Bulldogs by a combined eight points. Not surprisingly, in 1929, Poly had a new coach—one who would push the team to even greater heights than Kienholz had.

THE EARTHQUAKE AND BEYOND: ORIAN LANDRETH, 1929–1937

Orian Landreth's road to Poly was long and winding. Born and raised in a farmhouse in Macksville, Kansas, his father gave him the nickname "Toad" because of the way he hopped while still an infant. He was raised on the long, hard work of his father's wheat farm, but he left the rural life behind for college. One of a new breed of coaches who saw football as a mental exercise as much as a physical one, he majored in coaching and spent a year at the University of Illinois studying the schemes of Knute Rockne, poring over them like poetry.

He came to Southern California for a job at a middle school in San Diego and, after a few years as a Poly assistant, got the head coaching job in 1929, a post he held for nine seasons (the longest tenure to that point) before leaving to become the head coach of the University of Arizona. Later, he returned to Long Beach to coach and teach at Long Beach City College and refereed NCAA football for thirty-three years, including four Rose Bowl games. While at Poly, Landreth developed a reputation as a brilliant tactician and a supreme developer of talent.

He never once cursed at one of his players, though his growl became legendary, according to a *Los Angeles Times* article. Landreth's Poly teams became known as the "Giants of Atlantic Avenue," playing under the Landreth motto, "The team that won't be beaten, can't be beaten."

It was a sentiment that rang true in his first year, as Poly won its fourth CIF championship as the capper to a 7–0–3 season. Norm "Red" Franklin was the captain, leading the team to redemption against Pasadena in a 21–0 win to clinch the Coast League title. Franklin, a redhead, was an unstoppable freight train of a running back, carrying his team to the championship game by scoring the only touchdown in a 7–6 victory over Huntington Park in the semifinals. (He went on to All-American honors at Oregon State and had a brief pro career with the Brooklyn Dodgers football team).

Poly's Burcham Field was host to that year's championship against Santa Barbara. Over ten thousand fans crowded onto the campus field and had

A team shot of Poly's 1929 CIF championship squad. *Poly yearbook.*

barely settled in their seats when Bob Parke of the Jackrabbits picked off the opening pass and returned it seventy yards for the game's first touchdown, giving Poly a lead it never relinquished and giving Landreth his first championship.

Landreth's ever-evolving offense and relentless dedication to making men out of his young charges gave the team unprecedented success. In 1930, the team went 9–1 and became the first in history to win back-to-back Southern California championships. Franklin continued to star at running back and was the driving force in a 27–0 victory over Pasadena that evened the rivals' record with each other at 10–10–1. In the championship that year, the supremely conditioned Jackrabbits played Redondo and "ran the Seahawks ragged," according to one newspaper report. Orian Landreth was two for two as head coach, and Poly had won five championships. A bright future was in front of them.

Although Poly graduated all of its top talent from its 1929 and 1930 title teams, the losing seasons that followed in 1931 and 1932 were still considered disappointments by Jackrabbits fans. The 1932 season may have seen some team fatigue caused by the Summer Olympic games, which was held in Los Angeles and Long Beach that year. Several Poly players volunteered at the games. The Depression was in full swing at that point, and Landreth took great pride in continuing to get scholarships for his football players whose families could not have even dreamed of sending them to USC or Cal by other means.

The 1933 Long Beach Earthquake destroyed almost all of the city's schools, including its oldest high school, Long Beach Poly. *Poly yearbook.*

On March 10, 1933, however, on-field disappointments quickly fell by the wayside. At 5:55 p.m., Landreth had just left his house to referee a basketball game when the world went sideways; a 6.4 magnitude earthquake ripped up the Newport-Inglewood fault, which runs beneath the city. The epicenter was just off-shore, but the damage was devastating: 230 buildings were destroyed, including almost all of the city's schools, and 120 people were killed. Landreth was able to return home just in time to save his infant daughter from becoming one of the casualties.

By 6:05 p.m. that day, Long Beach was a city changed forever. Over $50 million in property damage had been done (an unimaginable amount of money in 1933), and Poly, the crown jewel in the city's proud and expanding school system, had been leveled. Only two buildings still stood on the historic campus. One of Poly's offensive linemen, according to a legend retold in the book *Art Deco Long Beach*, made his way to the hospital and spent forty-eight solid hours carrying water pails without spilling a drop.

When school opened in the fall of that year, Poly students went to class in a large tent city erected around the edges of Burcham Field. Players practiced and played just a few feet away from where they took English and math classes. Principal Burcham wrote, "In the coming year a new Polytechnic will rise from the ruins of the old. It will be made possible through the vision and foresight of the citizens of Long Beach." Although he was talking about architecture, he was also talking about the football team. The Jackrabbits went 6–3–1 that year, returning to their winning ways and giving exhausted Long Beach residents, who were spending every other moment rebuilding the city, something to cheer for.

The next year, though, the modern Poly campus was born. As Burcham wrote:

> *The past two years represent the most interesting period in all our school history. Three thousand students in tent houses, a regular school on a full-time schedule with every department functioning efficiently. Most important of all, in meeting a great emergency a new spirit has been born. The challenge to carry on in the face of physical handicaps and curtailed facilities has developed strength, self-reliance, and resourcefulness. New buildings are rising on the campus. We are beginning to have visions of a magnificent school plant to house the Polytechnic of the future. But we shall be a great school only in the measure in which we carry forward in that spirit which has risen to its greatest heights during the emergency period.*

Poly, rising from the ashes. The school rebuilds after the earthquake. *Poly yearbook.*

Hope was alive at Poly, where practices rang with the sounds of nearby construction, and where the football team decided to take out its frustrations by beating the hell out of any team that dared to step on the field with them. Bob Berryman starred as the quarterback, and Walter Ray McCowen was the star running back. McCowen was the first black football player at Poly, several decades before the rest of the country would be forced to integrate. After his time at Poly, he would discover that the rest of the world was not so forward-thinking as his high school, as he was rejected from employment by the Long Beach Police Department for "failing a blood test," coded language that meant he was turned down because of his race.

At Poly, though, McCowen's race didn't mean anything to his classmates, so long as he was working with them in service of the ideals of Poly, ideals that the earthquake had made even more vital. At Poly, McCowen was elected to student government and was an excellent student. On the field, he was a terror, scoring the only touchdown in a win against Poly's new crosstown rival, Long Beach Wilson High, which had begun playing Poly in 1932. In a game against San Diego that ended up deciding the league title, he ripped off an eighty-three-yard touchdown, shocking fans who were still used to a "three yards and a cloud of dust" style of offense.

With their city's name on their chests and their pride pushing them forward, the Jackrabbits took their 11–1 record into the LA Coliseum that

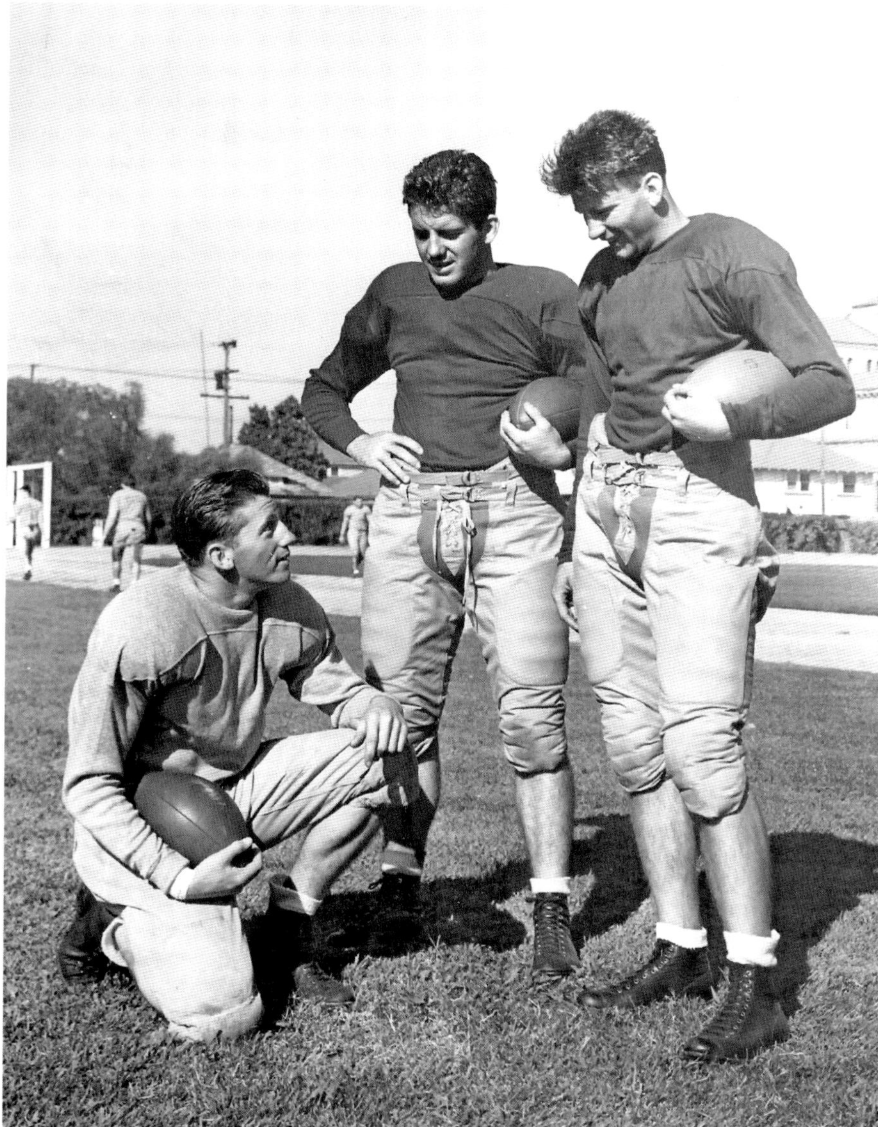

The Berryman brothers. All three starred at Poly together and went on to play at USC. *Courtesy* Press-Telegram.

year to face off against Chaffey for the CIF championship. Wilbur Ingram threw the only two touchdowns of the game, a twenty-one-yard strike to Fred Goodman and a twenty-three-yard score to Vic Elliot. Poly won 14–0.

Among those getting their rings was Jim Lineberger, who would go on to help get the city's iconic football stadium built and to coach at Long Beach Wilson. Berryman, one of the finest quarterbacks Long Beach had produced, went on to play at USC along with his fellow Jackrabbits and brothers, Cliff and Dick. Landreth would remember Berryman as one of the best players he ever coached. The Jackrabbits' statement was loud and clear: they were not going to be knocked down by anything, whether it be the thorny issue of race in a changing world or a 6.4 earthquake.

The year 1935 can be added to Poly's long register of lost championship seasons. The Jackrabbits were widely recognized as the best team in Southern California that year and ran their winning streak to eighteen games in a row, one of those a 20–13 win over eventual CIF champ Santa Barbara. But the Coast League, which Poly was a member of, decided to host a league carnival instead of participating in the playoffs. A tight-lipped Landreth referred to the decision as a "league alignment problem," which kept the Jackrabbits from defending their title, despite posting just the second all-win schedule in school history.

Burcham Field played host to the league carnival, which saw the league's different teams split up and form new alliances. In the first quarter, it was Santa Ana/San Diego v. Poly/Alhambra, with teams switching sides after each quarter. It was a fun enough exercise perhaps, but it cost the Jackrabbits a shot at the postseason. Perhaps as an apology, the normally eleven-man All-Coast League team was released...with twelve Jackrabbits on it.

The next year, though, the Jackrabbits won their seventh CIF title, which happened to be Landreth's fourth, a record that no coach has ever broken at Poly (although two have tied it). Poly was just 4–2–1 in the regular season that year but turned it on for the playoffs, beating Santa Barbara 23–7, El Monte 21–0 and blanking Glendale in the CIF championship game at the Rose Bowl with a score of 21–0. The Wilson rivalry was beginning to escalate, as the Bruins scored their first-ever touchdown against the Jackrabbits (though Poly still won).

Further demonstrating the serious consideration that Landreth brought to coaching decisions, he let Poly's record twenty-three-game winning streak lapse against Loyola, when he played nothing but subs in the mid-season game, wary of his already worn-down starters taking injuries or getting overly tired before the title run. He was criticized for the decision, naturally.

Ladusky McCowen, the first black quarterback in Poly and Long Beach history. He was the younger brother of Walter Ray McCowen, the school's first black player. *Poly yearbook.*

But running back Bob Blackman and the rest of the team appreciated the break and made the best of it, winning the league title and then sprinting to the championship.

Blackman went on to captain the USC freshman team before polio cut his playing career short. Having caught the coaching bug from Landreth, he then began a thirty-four-year coaching career while still an undergrad at USC, doing stints at Denver, Dartmouth, Illinois and Cornell. His 104–37–3 record at Dartmouth is what earned him his membership into the College Football Hall of Fame, a stretch that included three undefeated seasons and a Walter Camp Coach of the Year Award. Blackman helped promote such revolutionary ideas as allowing his players to drink water during practice.

Landreth had come into Poly with a bang, winning titles in his first two campaigns, but he went out with a whimper as Poly went 7–2 and was bounced from the playoffs in the first round, defeated by its old rival, Santa Ana, 15–12. When he left, the school had officially risen from the ashes; construction had left Poly looking much better than before the earthquake, with a state-of-the-art cafeteria and other new buildings filling in for the rubble that had been there just a few years before.

His final Jackrabbits team made a little bit more history, too. The issue of black quarterbacks in the NFL is still a favorite topic for ESPN talking heads to kick around, but for the Jackrabbits seventy-five years ago, it was an accepted fact. Ladusky McCowen (the younger brother of Walter Ray) was the first black signal-caller in Southern California, popular among his teammates and the team's fans. He helped keep Poly's streak against Wilson intact with a 21–0 victory on Armistice Day, in a game played in front of 14,000 fans.

And though the Jackrabbits bid Landreth farewell as he moved on to other coaching and refereeing gigs, his legacy lived on. As his former player Jim Lineberger told the *Press-Telegram*'s Bob Keisser, Landreth's philosophy was too simple to not hang onto. "All he wanted out of everybody was their best all the time," Lineberger recalled. "He used to say, 'Champions sometimes lose, but Champions never stop trying.'"

Poly certainly never stopped trying—but it would be twenty-two years before it would reach the top of the CIF mountain again.

THE DROUGHT: 1937–1957

The longest championship drought in the history of Long Beach Poly began with the long, drab tenure of Maxson "Red" Montgomery, who served thirteen years as a well-liked coach and was never fitted for a CIF ring. That's the longest stretch of service at the school without winning a title by nearly triple. At first, things appeared fine. Poly went 8–0 in Montgomery's first year, traveling to Arizona for a rematch with Phoenix High, a game Poly won by three touchdowns in front of a crowd of 12,000. The rivalry with Wilson was officially becoming lucrative for both schools, despite the Bruins' inability to beat their rivals. Poly beat Wilson 19–0 in 1938, in front of a crowd of over 30,000 at the Rose Bowl.

But things quickly began to fall apart. In Montgomery's second year, the school was barely over .500, with the uninspiring record of 3–2–2. The team lost to Phoenix in a rematch and barely beat Wilson, the final score being 7–0. The next year, Principal David Burcham left after thirty-four years at the helm of the school. America wasn't involved yet, but the Second World War was going strong in Europe, casting a dim light over such frivolities as school dances and football.

Starring on the 1940 team was a young man who would become an institution at the school, Sam Dimas. Dimas graduated and went on to a decorated career at Long Beach City College (LBCC), where he was voted student body president, and then to a decorated military career, winning the Purple Heart and Bronze Star as an army squad leader during the storming of Normandy. After finishing his collegiate eligibility at UC Santa Barbara, Dimas returned to Poly, where he taught and coached for thirty-seven years. Even after his retirement, he maintained close contact with the school and was instrumental as a link to the school's past, particularly during the recent creation of the Poly Football Hall of Fame.

Dimas's senior year, in 1940, Poly had an undefeated season (which included a come-from-behind win over Wilson), but the Jackrabbits were shocked by Whittier in the first round of the playoffs, losing 12–0 thanks to a host of fumbles, interceptions and costly penalties. The old Poly poise was lacking under Montgomery, and events the following year would put regaining it very, very low on the list of priorities.

In 1941, the Jackrabbits featured the brotherly tandem of Royal and Sam Cathcart, who came to Poly to follow in the footsteps of Dimas, their idol. The two went on to great things. Sam was signed with the San Francisco 49ers and was named rookie of the year at the start of a five-year tenure with the team. He was recalled into active duty for the Korean War, which cut a promising career short.

In 1941, Poly again beat its crosstown rivals, Wilson, by the score of 12–6, on November 29. It was the last game played that year; Japan attacked Pearl Harbor eight days later. During World War II, the Poly ROTC's ranks swelled, and the ranks of everything else shrank. Long Beach was a navy town and was considered an attractive target on the Pacific coast for America's enemies, so a sense of heightened awareness filled citizens' everyday routines. It was difficult to go to Recreation Park and enjoy a baseball game, for example, when the tops of the trees that ringed the outfield wall had been chopped to make room for huge antiaircraft guns.

Poly muddled on, but the losses were staggering. And not just on the field—kids were graduating and going straight to Europe or the Pacific Theatre. The oasis of peace and tolerance that Poly had represented was warped into a machine, churning out students for World War II. In the yearbooks, pictures of smiling students were replaced with grim portraits of serious, determined young men and women. So many Poly alumni were killed within a few years of graduating that the yearbooks of the time feature updated lists of fallen Poly soldiers.

A memorial service was held on campus, filling the quad with mourners. The principal promised a War Memorial Library, as a way of paying permanent tribute to those lost forever. The concerns of the football team, of course, seemed trivial in comparison. In 1943, the team went 1–4–1, one of just four times in school history that it would win one or fewer games. The

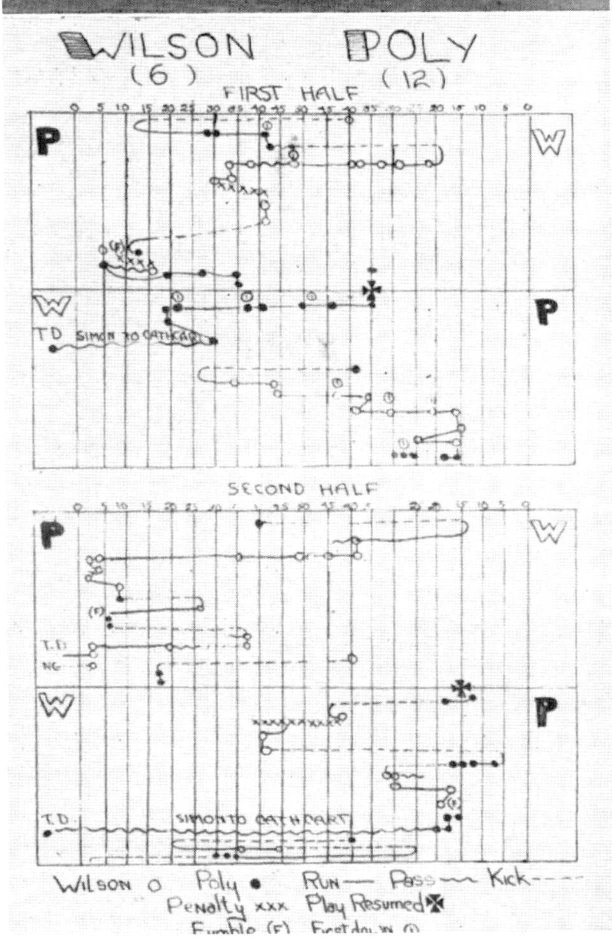

Drive chart from the 1941 Poly v. Wilson game, which was played just eight days before the attack on Pearl Harbor. *Poly yearbook.*

The 1945 World War II Memorial Service for slain soldiers from Long Beach. There were many. *Poly yearbook.*

team lost its first-ever game to Wilson, 37–7, a moment that lives in Bruins fans' memories to this day. The next season, the school held a half-hearted fiftieth anniversary celebration, but there wasn't much celebrating going on in America at that point.

The fall of 1945 brought with it good news on the war front, as the Second World War ended in September of that year. But the team was stuck in neutral, going 4–4 that fall and missing the playoffs yet again. This time the Jackrabbits didn't just lose to Wilson but also to another new high school in the city as well: Long Beach Jordan. The mediocrity prevented great players of the time from entering into Poly's championship pantheon, though they went on to distinguish themselves at the next level.

Bill Jessup was an All-CIF player who won All-American honors at LBCC, played at USC and then spent seven years in the NFL with the 49ers and the Broncos. He was the eleventh Jackrabbit to enter the pro ranks, officially giving them a starting side. George van Zant was the star running back in 1949, the last winning season that Montgomery would muster. Van Zant went on to a successful career at LBCC and would become a magazine and newspaper writer in his later life, including penning a popular outdoors and fishing column in the *Press-Telegram*.

Another star of the time was Dave Levy, who was apparently so sick of seeing Poly struggle that, a few years later, he came back to do something about it. The Jackrabbits/Bruins games continued to draw more than ten thousand fans as the area's premier rivalry. With a total dearth of postseason success, that was the only game where Poly players got to really experience the thrill of the big stage. As if things couldn't get worse, in 1949, the center bleachers at Burcham Field, which had stood for decades, were irreparably burned in a fire.

Montgomery closed his tenure in 1951 with a 1–7 season, losing 13–12 to Wilson in the first game played at Long Beach's new field, Veterans Memorial Stadium, constructed in honor of the many Long Beach citizens who had lost their lives in World War II. Outside of football, things were bright on campus. Poly was building new gymnasiums, a new natatorium and the War Memorial Library, designed by principal Howard Hicks, making good on his promise.

Realizing he had achieved all he was going to be able to, Montgomery tendered his resignation, which Hicks accepted remorsefully. Montgomery remained popular, largely above the criticism that usually falls on the shoulders of a Poly coach, win or lose. "He's had his hard knocks with illness and injuries to key players on years when things looked rather bright," said Hicks. "And we have not been unaware of them."

In came poor Cal Rossi, who coached three losing seasons, becoming the only coach in Poly history to coach multiple seasons without ever posting a winning record. Rossi had NFL-level talent, including Gerry McDougall (an All-American at UCLA who spent a decade in the pro ranks, including three seasons with the Chargers), Johnny Morris (still the Chicago Bears' all-time leading receiver in yardage and touchdowns) and Henry Wallace, who also spent time with the Bolts in San Diego. But it was to no avail, as the team went 3–5, 2–6 and 1–5–1 in Rossi's final year.

The school next turned to Doc Cure, a Judo instructor for the Marines who had played pro ball with the Colts and who was also a math teacher on campus. Seeking to return the school to its rightful place among the best, Cure tried motivational quotes, boasting to the media, "I'm not coming to Poly to lose all my games." True to his word, he won two of them, going 2–5–1 in his first season, losing to Wilson, Jordan and Compton. The next year, 1956, the Jackrabbits did indeed finish 5–3, their first winning season since 1949. For the first time in seven years, they beat both Wilson and Jordan. Also that year, the team lost its first Super Fan; "Pop" Hyde was ninety years old and had attended almost every Poly game ever. He passed away, earning recognition from the school and the team.

Lonzo McGlothern, a small but mighty football and track star, who passed away before a track meet on campus. *Courtesy* Press-Telegram.

With the tough-minded Cure failing to flip Poly's fortune, the school's administration turned to one of its own, Poly and UCLA graduate Dave Levy. Levy had been an assistant under Cure and, when Cure stepped down from the job, Levy put his name in the running. "They looked at everyone, some bigger names, and they didn't get them for whatever reason," Levy remembered. "Some time in May, Neil Philips, the principal, just asked me—'Do you really want this job?' I said, 'Yes.' He said, 'You got it.' I was twenty-five years old."

Levy was also on LBCC's 1950 national championship team, bringing an impressive Long Beach pedigree with him to his alma mater. Bill Mulligan served as backfield coach, a good idea as the Jackrabbits would be known for unstoppable running backs for the next few years. Mulligan became "the brain behind the seemingly impossible backfield maneuvers" executed by the team in those years, according to one yearbook account.

The team wasn't quite ready to compete for a championship yet, but its 6–1–1 record in 1957, Levy's first season, was its best record in almost a decade. That year saw the formation of the Moore League, named for Poly and Wilson administrator Harry J. Moore, the league that Poly has been in ever since. The opening of Millikan and Lakewood High Schools made the new league possible, as it allowed the Long Beach schools to play each other. The lone loss that season came to Wilson, keeping Poly from winning the Moore League's first title and keeping the team from making the playoffs that year.

The Jackrabbits' most difficult loss that year wasn't to the Bruins, however. Lonzo McGlothern was just 5'6" and 135 pounds, but he had a reputation for being unstoppable on the football field. He was bright, well liked and a multisport athlete, playing football and basketball and running hurdles in track. In the spring of his senior year, he collapsed and died on the field before a track meet, the result of a heart condition. The *Press-Telegram*, familiar with his brand of reckless, awe-inspiring football, said that he was a "victim of his own fighting spirit."

But as had been the case before, the tragedy didn't break the Jackrabbits—instead, it galvanized them, and the drought would end in a brief shower of CIF championship hardware the next two years.

A Return: Dave Levy, 1958–1959

The next two seasons were almost unfair to Poly's competition. With the young, energetic Levy coaching the team and the best running backs you could ever hope to see, the Jackrabbits regained their swagger and their winning ways. In 1958 and 1959, they went a combined 22–0–1, winning two CIF championships, the eighth and ninth in school history.

In 1958, Dee Andrews and Willie Brown both starred as running backs. Andrews went on to win a national championship at Long Beach City College, followed by a successful career at Long Beach State. In this, his senior year, he rushed for 1,330 yards in just eight games, while splitting time with Brown, a splendid back in his own right who went on to a great career at USC and with the Los Angeles Rams. Andrews earned CIF Player of the Year honors and won state track titles in the high hurdles and long jump. In recent years, Andrews has remained a fixture at Poly games and events. He currently serves as Long Beach's city councilman for the sixth district, where the school is located.

The 1958 season started with five straight wins, none of them closer than two scores. After suffering a 7–7 tie with Colton, Poly closed the regular season with a pair of blowout wins over Moore League newbies Lakewood and Millikan. The team had looked strong the previous year, too, but hadn't had a chance to test its mettle in the postseason—it was the playoffs where it would have to prove itself.

In the first round, the Jackrabbits looked like they might stumble. They were tied at 13 points apiece with North Torrance, with just two seconds left in the game. At that time, the number of first downs a team had gained was used as the tie-breaker, so with Poly trailing 10–6 in that category, the Jackrabbits needed a score to win the game. The ball went back to Willie Brown, who set up and sent a prayer downfield. Bobby Banks managed to grab it, scoring a fifty-five-yard Hail Mary touchdown that won the game and gave Poly life. Long after he graduated, Banks would tell some of his teammates that he had actually been out of bounds when he caught it—a rare moment in history when a bad officiating call *benefitted* the Jackrabbits. That game ended in a huge bench-clearing brawl when one of the Torrance players took a cheap shot at a Poly player, but the Jackrabbits got away unscathed.

The next round, they dispatched San Diego Union on the road but lost Andrews to injury in a stadium filled with over thirteen thousand fans. "They blacked out the stadium," Mike Giers, the team's all-star right tackle, remembered. "All the lights were out except a few, and we're on the ground

Lynn Hoyem and Dee Andrews. Hoyem and Andrews played together at Long Beach State. *Courtesy* Press-Telegram.

getting ready. And then all these candles from the top of the stadium were lit and they came walking down the steps. Our line coach Don Hardy, I've never heard a coach cuss like that. He was a minister, and they made it look like they were coming down from heaven to beat us." Poly won 26–18.

On a team as deep as Poly's that year, even losing a star like Andrews couldn't slow the Jackrabbits down. Transfer Willie Martin stepped in to assist Brown, and Poly thumped Colton (which had tied the Jackrabbits earlier in the year) 41–27 in the semifinals, advancing to the championship against Santa Monica.

"Practices at that time were intense," laughs Giers. He recalled one in particular involving the sophomore running back, Harvey Crow. "Crow kept messing up in practice, and Dave Levy told him, 'If you screw up one more time, I'm going to kick you right in the balls.' He screwed up, and Harvey got down in a stance, and Levy kicked him right in the ass!"

The championship was to be played at the Los Angeles Coliseum, on a field so torn up by that point that the grounds crew painted it green to engage spectators in the fantasy that there was still some grass cover. While the players were getting ready to go to the game, members of the neighborhood came up and got autographs. Andrews laughs, remembering. "Someone had me sign an orange. I didn't know anything about signing autographs, and they didn't know anything about getting them." In front of an announced crowd of 14,152, it was Brown's turn to step up. The junior gained 106 yards on 17 carries and scored four touchdowns in the 31–19 Poly win.

Throughout the season, Poly's linemen were spectacular. Todd Jagerson was named to the first-team All-CIF list and Jim Smith was an All-American, called "one of the finest linemen in team history" by TEEN magazine. Smith played a season with the New York Giants after starring for LBCC and USC, a familiar pattern for Jackrabbits of the Levy era.

What set the teams of the time apart was their great affection for each other, a sentiment that the players interviewed for this book all share. Many of them still keep in touch more than fifty years later. "We were a family," said Andrews. "Dave Levy and Bill Mulligan made it that way. We never had a moment of racism on that team, we melted in with each other like a family."

In the late fifties, it was still significant for an integrated football team to not experience racial strife, though it had been almost thirty years since Poly had first had black players on the field. There were still big parts of Long Beach off-limits to African Americans—not just areas to live in but also areas to even visit. On campus, though, those lines didn't exist.

"I saw that movie *Remember the Titans,*" said Giers. "And I said, 'Jesus that was us, but we were ten years earlier.' I remember Lonzo Irvin came over to my house [in Bixby Knolls]. He came and knocked on the door, and all these people were looking out their windows at this black guy knocking. And my mother looked and saw all these neighbors, and she says, 'What are you looking at? It's just Lonzo Irvin!' There was just something there with those three years—they were really special."

The next year, there were a few different faces but almost the exact same story. This time, the Jackrabbits improved on their 11–0–1 mark by going 11–0, with Brown, Martin, Lonzo Irvin and Harvey Crow, splitting carries out and earning the group's backfield position the explosive nickname "ICBM." That group was so good (regarded as four of the best five backs in all of the CIF), it actually garnered multiple nicknames. Another paper dubbed them the "Magic" backfield. As for how that name came to be, take your pick: was it that their feet were faster than the eye or because those four players had a tendency to make defenders disappear?

Either way, the four of them averaged a combined 484 yards per game on the ground. "Wee" Willie Brown set a school record with 1,784 yards in his senior season, averaging 13.5 yards per carry and scoring 22 touchdowns, earning him state player of the year honors. Brown went on to win a national championship with USC and launched his NFL career with the Rams and Eagles.

As you might imagine, a backfield that talented had plenty of support. Not only was Mulligan still the designated coach of the platoon (doing some hustling himself that year, as he also coached the basketball team to a CIF title), but the linemen were stellar as well. Chief among them was "Big" Mike Giers, a fireplug of a right tackle with an open smile who turned into a warrior on the field. He was named All-American and went on to star at LBCC and USC before signing with the New York Giants in 1965. A total of five NFL players came off the two Poly championship rosters.

That 1959 team couldn't be touched, because none of the players could be caught. Nobody was within two touchdowns of them for the entire season. In the Jackrabbits' final seven games, nobody could stay within three scores, and their total tally for the year was 420–118. The running backs were so good that Giers recalled Levy telling the offensive line, "Once they get through the line of scrimmage, all I want you to do is stand there and clap. You're not going to catch them to try and block downfield anyway." The Jackrabbits opened with a 40–0 win over Paso Robles and just kept rolling from there. Their biggest crowd all year was at Veterans Memorial Stadium

Willie Brown, getting an equipment assist from classmate June Shinoi. *Courtesy* Press-Telegram.

"Big" Mike Giers, an all-star offensive lineman. Poly coach Dave Levy is on his left and LBCC coach Jim Stangeland on his right. *Courtesy* Press-Telegram.

(Vets, or The Vet to those who know it) to watch them play Wilson in the Big Game, which didn't seem quite that big in 1959. Poly won 35–13, as Brown scored touchdowns of 90, 70 and 33 yards. By the time the playoffs rolled around, Poly was as confident as could be—the Jackrabbits were riding an unbeaten streak that would eventually extend to 25 games.

In the playoff opener against Montebello, Poly scored 50 points. The next week against Mt. Carmel, it was the modest total of 40. The championship was almost anticlimactic as the rest of Southern California wasn't ready to challenge them. In front of almost 15,000 fans at the Coliseum, the

Fans celebrate Poly's 1959 CIF championship. *Poly yearbook.*

Jackrabbits blew by Hawthorne 42–20. Jack Hefley for the *Los Angeles Times* wrote, "Bone-crushing Long Beach Poly buried Hawthorne under a deluge of touchdowns to coast to the CIF championship." Brown had a 48-yard touchdown, but Lonzo Irvin took his day in the sun, with 125 yards and a pair of scores in the first half. "The Coliseum crowd went home convinced that Poly could take any high school team in the state, if not the nation, to task," wrote Hefley. With the wealth of talent on those rosters, it's hard to argue with him.

In the modern landscape of high school football, Levy would probably have been hired away after that season by a deep-pocketed private high school. In those days, USC (and not prep Catholic schools) was the private school with the money to do it. It snatched Levy up, and he served as an assistant to John McKay from 1960 to 1975, helping to keep the Jackrabbit pipeline to the Trojans open and continuing a lifelong coaching career. (In 2011, Levy coached with Harvard-Westlake, and he'll be the quarterbacks coach for Fairfax in 2012). Levy's time at USC is an incredible snapshot of Southern California football history—he was there when Poly's Willie Brown was hired as USC's first-ever black coach, and he was there for the USC/Alabama game where Sam Cunningham so impressed Bear Bryant that the Alabama coach decided to integrate his program. After that, he went on to a pro career, reaching the heights of assistant head coach of the Detroit Lions in the early 1990s.

"When you win like [we did at Poly], it's not coaching, it's really not—it's players," said Levy. "I ran a good program, but the players were there. We also had the greatest athletic principal of all time. Neil Philips would actually film games for us because he knew a good football team was good for morale."

Levy also said, despite an attachment to his alma mater, he didn't have to think about it for very long when USC called. "Look, if USC calls, USC calls. If you could only coach where you went to school, there wouldn't be that many people coaching. It just doesn't work that way."

It's hard to believe that Levy was able to take the reins at Poly at the young age of twenty-five and wring two championships in three years out of his alma mater. But a lifetime of coaching, with championships never far from hand, showed that Levy had the gift—and for three years, he shared it with the school and the city that helped make him. His departure would bring about the second-longest championship drought in Poly's history, as well as the program's lowest points.

THINGS FALL APART: 1960–1979

Over the next twenty years, Poly would cycle through seven coaches and forfeit games over ineligible players twice. The school and its surrounding area would also be completely torn apart by racial strife, to the extent that Poly was almost seized by the federal government and closed. In the early 1960s, though, that trouble must have seemed a universe away. Poly was still turning out Divison 1 athletes who would go on to successful NFL careers, and the team almost certainly had yet another championship stolen from them.

The first coach to try his hand at following the championship legacies of Landreth and Levy was Maury Ross. Jackrabbits fans, ever impatient, were frustrated with the first two efforts as Poly not only failed to defend its CIF titles, but also lost the Moore League title to Wilson twice in a pair of fantastic games decided by a total of six points. In 1961, though, the team went 8–2, with its only loss of the regular season coming to the Bruins, followed by an upset second-round playoff loss to El Rancho. The next year, the team again went 8–2, this time edging Wilson by a touchdown, but once again losing in the second round, this time to Redlands. That year, Poly principal Neil Philips opened the school's hall of fame, suspended over the main entrance and used as a walkway between the 300 and 400 buildings on campus—but no extra space was left for the team fielded that year.

The next year should have been different, though. In 1963, Mulligan, the architect of the backfields of the late 1950s and a legendary basketball coach in his own right, spent a single season as head coach of the football squad. If it hadn't been for a CIF playoff scandal, he could perhaps have extended the school's run of dominance a bit deeper into the 1960s.

The Jackrabbits team that year featured a pair of future NFL stars, quarterback Gene Washington and running back Earl "The Pearl" McCullouch. There was other excellent talent, as well—players like Al Nichols, Marv Motley and Elwood Stewart, but Washington and McCullouch were about as good a 1–2 punch as you'd ever hope to see on a high school football team.

McCullouch, at the time, was probably the most talented athlete to ever come out of the school. While in high school, he set national records in the high hurdles and low hurdles, winning two state track championships while also starring on the football team. He'll forever be the world record holder in the eighteen-yard low hurdles, as the event is no longer run. He also held a world record in the 110-meter high hurdles for three years. After winning a national championship with LBCC in 1964, he and O.J. Simpson helped propel USC to a national title in 1967, before being drafted by the Detroit Lions in the first round, eventually winning NFL Rookie of the Year honors at the beginning of a long tenure with the Lions and Saints.

Washington, who was just a junior in 1963, starred at Poly as a quarterback but was eventually moved to wide receiver at Stanford, a position he learned

Earl McCullouch, one of the finest athletes ever turned out by Poly. *Courtesy* Press-Telegram.

pretty well—well enough, at least, to be named All-American. Perhaps more important than his on-field contributions, he was a trailblazer at the school, one of just twenty-five African American students at a campus of ten thousand students when he enrolled. While there, he became the second black member of the Delta Tau Delta fraternity. His classmates at Poly were not surprised, of course: Washington was the first black student body president at the high school. Later in life, he would become the first black member of the Los Angeles Country Club, and *Sports Illustrated* would name him one of the "101 Most Influential Minorities in Sports" in 2004.

Out of Stanford, Washington was drafted eighteenth overall by the San Francisco 49ers, coming into the league a year after his old teammate, McCullouch. He wasn't named rookie of the year, but he was a four-time NFL Pro Bowler during his nine-year stretch with the 49ers, hauling in sixty touchdown catches, all the while maintaining a side career as an actor in movies and television. After retiring from football following the 1979 season, Washington was an NFL commentator with NBC in the early 1980s. From 1994 to 2009 he worked for the league, serving as its director of football operations in charge of all fines and suspensions and, occasionally, doling out punishments to the almost twenty graduates of his old high school who entered the league during his watch.

All of that is a long way to a short point: Poly was good in 1963. The team blew through its nonleague schedule and suffered through the only game it didn't win that year against Wilson, tying 20–20. That game was one of just two times in the ten-game schedule that Poly's high-powered offense failed to score at least four touchdowns.

After defeating Santa Ana in an easy first-round game, the mighty Jackrabbits took a 9–0–1 record and a lot of hard-earned confidence into their quarterfinal game against El Rancho. Mulligan contacted Aaron Wade, the head coach of Centennial, and requested film of El Rancho, which he received. In the current world of the CIF, teams are actually required to exchange film before playoff games, and refusal to do so can result in disqualification. In 1963, due to a brand new rule, however, Mulligan had just sealed a terrible fate for his team.

The Jackrabbits won handily, 27–0. But CIF Southern Section commissioner Ken Fagans had the unenviable task of later informing Poly that an easy quarterfinal victory would actually be Poly's last game of the year. Mulligan said that he was unaware of the new bylaw that prohibited viewing other teams' game film and begged the CIF to punish him in any way it saw fit, but not his championship-caliber team. Fagans and the CIF ruled

Gene Washington in action. *Courtesy* Press-Telegram.

that Poly's win was forfeit and that the team was done. In an interview with Jeff Frugh for the *Los Angeles Times*, Fagans admitted somewhat sheepishly, "Actually this was the first week the rule was put into effect."

Frugh and the other prep experts of the time were stunned. "Poly didn't need films," he wrote. "They were unsurpassed even by the championship teams of the Willie Brown and Dee Andrews era...this is a thundering blow to the LBP team and its followers."

"It was disappointing," said Poly assistant Don Norford, a player on that year's team and a coach since 1976. "The whole campus was sad. And we were upset because all the other teams were doing it. But as soon as it looked like we were going to win a championship, two coaches turned us in."

It was a blow so thundering that Washington and McCullouch would still bring it up decades later. While the CIF can't necessarily be blamed for following the letter of a bizarre, quickly outdated rule, Poly can't be blamed for imagining the championship that should have been but wasn't, the fifth such year in the school's history (along with 1918, 1920, 1921 and 1935). Mulligan was so heartbroken to have hurt his players' chance at a championship that he turned his clipboard over to Al Matz, who would coach the team for the next five years.

Things hummed along for the first year. Washington was still under center, and the very capable Nichols was now the starting running back. The Jackrabbits led the CIF in scoring at 33 points per-game in 1964 and beat Wilson by 28, but their run was cut down by Whittier in the semifinals, despite leading in first downs and yardage and never punting. Nichols gained 177 yards in the game, but Poly turned the ball over too many times. The drop-off was immediate, as the team went 2–3 in the Moore League the next year and 4–5 overall, Poly's first losing record in a decade. In Matz's final four years, Poly didn't finish higher than third place in the Moore League. Yearbook summaries from those years began to contain such philosophical hand wringing as this passage: "There can be only one winner—but does that make all the rest losers?" For Poly fans, of course, the answer was yes.

Salvation was present, however, as Jerry Jaso became the best defensive back on the 1967 team. Jaso would return to Poly to become arguably the greatest coach in the team's history—but not for several years. Matz was replaced in 1969 by Phil Santia, who went 4–5 and 1–8 as a head coach, with a combined two-year Moore League record of 1–9. Poly finished fifth and dead last in the league it had once dominated and didn't even sniff the postseason. Even talent like Carl Weathers (more famous now as an actor, but who was also an NFL pro with the Raiders) went unused. Besides the occasional bright spot, the wells were running dry, and the luster was off the gold in the green and gold.

The world was changing around the campus, and 1600 Atlantic no longer represented the shining beacon of progressive thought it once had. In 1970, the school celebrated its seventy-fifth anniversary. In the celebrations, there were a lot of photos of trophies—none of them were new.

In the aftermath of the mid-60s Watts Riots, Long Beach turned into a city that had "a race problem." Always a gathering place for people of many nationalities and backgrounds, thanks to the Port of Long Beach and the Naval Base, different races began to clash over neighborhoods and territories.

Author Don Wallace, whose great-uncle and grandfather were among the first football players at Poly, remembered his days at Poly in the late 1960s in his book, *One Great Game*. The snack stand in the courtyard next to the school's quad, long a place of gathering, not only held breakfast foods in Wallace's time but also served as a site of two race riots, a problem that persisted. Here, he writes about the late 1960s and early '70s: "Swiftly, angrily, the social fabric frayed. By 1969 the school was in the heart of a ghetto. Violent riots in 1970 and 1972 shattered the campus. Federal authorities who arrived in the

Tony Hill at Stanford, where he followed in Gene Washington's shoes by switching from quarterback to receiver. *Courtesy* Press-Telegram.

aftermath of the riots publicly weighed taking over Poly. A proud city was left reeling." Camelot had fallen, and things were a long way from getting better.

Into that unenviable world stepped Troy Winslow, who had quarterbacked USC's Rose Bowl team in 1965. Winslow became the head coach in 1971, a year which once again saw Poly finish dead last in the Moore League. In 1972, there was a one-year revival, thanks almost entirely to Tony Hill. Hill was the star quarterback, who threw for over a thousand yards and ran for nearly five hundred, scoring fifteen touchdowns along the way. In 1972, he took the Jackrabbits to their first Moore League title since 1964, the longest ever drought for Poly in Moore League history. He also led them to their first postseason since '64, earning All-CIF honors after Poly's second-round ouster.

He went on to Stanford where he mirrored Gene Washington by moving to wide receiver, the position he would fill during his successful NFL career with the Cowboys. There was a nice rivalry between Hill and Washington, as Hill broke Washington's passing records at Poly and then his receiving records at Stanford. In the NFL, he spent a decade in Dallas, scoring fifty-one touchdowns and earning three NFL Pro Bowl nods. After the 8–3 season, things were looking up for the Jackrabbits—but they had no idea how bad things were about to get.

The Bottom: 1973

The year 1973 was unarguably the worst year in the history of Poly football. The landscape of the campus was continuing to change, and the area around the school continued to worsen. On the field, the football team failed to win a game for the first (and still only) time in team history, going 0–8 and scoring just 49 points. It was as though the wind had completely gone out of the school's once-billowing sails, and the football team, perhaps the whole campus, was languishing, going nowhere on a stillborn breeze.

"This will long be remembered as the season that should be forgotten," reads that season's yearbook. Worse than the on-field record was an ugly incident after a junior varsity game against Muir on Poly's campus. The Muir team was walking to board a bus after the game when players heard loud arguing from a nearby house. A shot rang out, exploding a glass window onto the Muir team, injuring one player. Another player, fifteen-year-old Richard Snowden, was struck by a bullet in the head. He clung to life at St. Mary's in

A haunting message from Poly's no-win 1973 season, in which the program bottomed out and a visiting player was murdered while walking to his team's bus. *Poly yearbook.*

Long Beach but did not survive. "It seems crass to even report about a season that ended in such a way," reads the yearbook. "Thus the opportunity to criticize coaches, players, referees, etc, will be passed."

A few years later, Poly's All-American running back Artie Hargrove (remembered by players and fans of the time as one of Poly's finest backs) hanged himself in his garage, apparently distraught over not having made the grades to accept a scholarship offer from UCLA. The Long Beach football community was shocked senseless.

Things could not get worse. The campus wasn't united, the community was almost at war with itself and (trivial as it may have seemed) the football team that had been the pride and the standard-bearer of both couldn't win a measly game. Football had once been a way of life in Long Beach. But high school athletes suddenly seemed engaged in a struggle between life and death. The once enormous crowds that had filled Vets to watch Poly play dried up and blew away. The affluent Bixby Knolls residents who had helped make up the school's history did not want to watch what they saw as a ghetto football team. Parents began to fear sending their kids to the school, worried about what the neighborhood and campus climate might become at any given moment. Long Beach's other high schools flourished as the racial demographics of the city became a burden instead of a blessing.

"I mean, it got bleak," said Jaso. "People always say, 'Well how could you lose at Poly?' And I say, 'There's people who did.'"

Steps were being taken to piece the school back together, and it definitively managed to remain out of the control of the federal government. But the efforts put forth wouldn't come to fruition for years. In the meantime, former assistant Mike Scarpace took over head coaching duties, having nowhere to go but up. He led the team to two winning records, one Moore League title and a pair of first-round playoff exits. Those meager offerings seemed like feasts at the time.

Gene Noji, still the first and only Japanese-American head coach at a school whose Japanese heritage and history run deep, was next to hoist the clipboard. He was the head coach from 1976 to 1979 and continued to help right the ship, even while struggling with racial unrest. In 1976, Poly formed the Inter-Racial Committee to have representatives from each race on campus help liaison with the community; community members had their own committee, as well, which came together to find solutions. The on-campus incarnation, which currently survives as the International Ambassadors, helped change the face of the school, as did the implementation of academic magnet programs like PACE and CIC, which remain two of California's best public school magnets. Peace on the campus and high-quality education helped bring the Bixby Knolls crowd back in and open the campus back up to students of all races.

The football team had four winning records and almost reached a championship peak in 1977, with receiver Chuckie Allen and end Wayne Nichols starring on the field. It finished fourth in the Moore League but made the playoffs as a wild card and, in the first round, upset top-seeded Santa Monica, 13–6. The team then went on to beat Thousand Oaks, 7–3, to set up a semifinal showdown with Moore League foe Millikan. The Rams prevailed, 27–7, but the Jackrabbits were officially back on track.

The next year, they would take the Moore League title again with a perfect record. In an unfortunate foreshadowing of things to come, they forfeited a victory over St. John Bosco for having used an ineligible player. In 1979, the team went 6–2–1 on the field but went 0–9 in the CIF ledger, following a ruling that said the team had used two ineligible players throughout. The Moore League rules stated that a transfer student must wait twenty weeks before he could play for his new school. Coach Noji said the two students in question had sat out the required time, but he lost a dispute over whether the start of those twenty weeks was on the transfer date or the beginning of the school year.

Still, things were looking up on campus. Other teams were winning CIF titles, and Poly had officially put the bulk of its turmoil behind it. It did it not by ignoring the issues, but, like a football team, by acknowledging its problems and tackling them head on, with programs like the Inter-Racial Committee and Poly North, a mountain retreat designed to promote racial interaction and understanding (also still being run at the school). Both of these celebrated their fifth anniversary in 1979. The yearbook from that year lists the twenty nationalities represented by the school's student body, as Poly entered a multi-decade stretch where it would represent America's most diverse high school, a distinction it holds to this day. A passage reads: "The students and faculty at Poly are united by a special bond. We are one. How can you tell? You can hear it when we win...and sense it when we've been defeated. The unity that we feel stems from sharing a common experience—the Poly experience."

While Ross, Mulligan, Matz, Santia, Winslow, Scarpace and Noji failed to deliver a title, they successfully steered Poly's football team through the most difficult patch in the school's history. That was no small feat—and had they failed, none of the success of the next thirty years would have been possible.

Every great tragedy or challenge in Poly's history has been marked by a resurgence of its football team. So it probably shouldn't have come as a surprise, as Poly left behind the racial turmoil of the late 1960s and '70s, that the Jackrabbits were about to get very, very good, and Southern California fans were about to "hear it" from the united Poly campus.

THE PRIDE RETURNS: JIM BARNETT, 1980–1984

Of the many great coaches that Poly has had, only three of them are in a Hall of Fame in the city of Long Beach: Landreth is in the Century Club's Hall of Fame; Jaso is in the Poly Football Hall of Fame, with four CIF rings; and Jim Barnett is the third. Barnett, a Lakewood graduate who hated that neither he nor his Lancer teammates ever got any awards because Poly players were soaking them up, became the defensive coordinator at Poly in 1975.

Though the head coach for five seasons, he won only one CIF championship. To Poly fans, though, it's the one that opened the floodgates

Coach Jim Barnett, who helped reestablish the championship tradition at Long Beach Poly. *Courtesy* Press-Telegram.

and restored the pride at the school, creating a new, modern legacy that's been going strong for three decades. There has been only one losing season since Barnett's first year at the school. "He got them back on their feet," said the *Press-Telegram*'s Bob Keisser.

The names on the 1980 roster were familiar to Poly fans: Stefan Derrick, Paul Ussery, Kirk Jones. The Jackrabbits started by beating Lynwood and St. Francis, then lost to Banning and beat Crespi to close out the preseason. A one-point win over Compton and a 9–8 loss to a mediocre Lakewood team threw postseason expectations into flux (the Lancers finished the year at 3–5–1), but this Poly team was made up of fighters. After losing to Lakewood, the Jackrabbits closed the season with seven straight wins, never scoring fewer than 23 points.

The Jackrabbits' hard-hitting, athletic style of play was thrilling, even if their skill level meant that the games usually weren't. It was around this time that college scouts began throwing around the phrase, "There's speed, and then there's *Poly* speed," as Dick Lascola mentioned in a *Sporting News* feature. The obvious class of the CIF, Barnett's Jackrabbits beat Crescenta Valley 26–8 in the first round and then brushed off North Torrance 24–3 in the second. They exploded offensively against Arcadia in the semifinals, beating them 56–21 by no-huddling a team that starred future NFL Hall of Fame lineman Bruce Matthews. "That was like, 'Boy, those Poly guys know what they're doing a little bit,'" said Barnett. That set up the title game against Santa Barbara, which was quarterbacked by future NFL star Randall Cunningham.

Starting linebacker A.J. Luke (who would return to coach the freshman team and, more recently, the varsity linebackers) served another role that night, taking the microphone to sing the national anthem before the game. After the song was over, the curtains dropped on Santa Barbara; Cunningham couldn't do anything against Joe Person and Paul Ussery's ferocious defense. Poly led 28–0 at halftime against the previously undefeated Dons and cruised to a 35–7 win, its first championship since 1959.

Barnett was a Lakewood guy, and he knew that unsettled a lot of the Poly community. "Fortunately, we won CIF so they forgave me for being a white guy from Lakewood," he laughs. "For a while, at least."

Thanks to the innovations of the school's administration, as well as the even-handed coaching style of Jim Barnett, the team was able to come together and reach for the CIF's golden ring. Outside of the campus, racial tension continued to flare. In 1981, Long Beach State running back Ron Settles was arrested in Signal Hill for speeding and died that night in his jail

Kirk Jones, the all-star running back, in action in 1981. *Poly yearbook.*

cell, severely beaten and hanged. The Signal Hill police, who had developed a reputation for harassing black Long Beach citizens who drove through their city, had to pay Settles' family $1 million as the result of a lawsuit launched from national outrage surrounding the incident.

Barnett was able to guide Poly back to the CIF championship the next two years but fell 21–8 to Santa Monica and 31–7 to Servite. After the long drought the school's fans had endured, just getting to the big game was nice, even if it was the first CIF championship that Poly had lost (the team was 10–0 to that point).

Kirk Jones starred on both the 1980 and 1981 teams as running back and linebacker and helped to establish the new mold of Poly athlete, one who was gifted with incredible physical talent but whom college coaches also knew would have his grades in order. In a bit of showmanship that would foreshadow the over-produced "signing day announcement" TV segments of today, Jones announced his college commitment over the PA system at the CIF championship game. His announcing he would be joining the University of Nevada at Las Vegas (UNLV) is still considered a seminal moment in that school's history. Jones went on to a brief NFL career with the Saints, Patriots and Browns before returning to Poly to coach.

Other NFL players on the championship loss teams were Dennis Price and Chuckie Miller, who went to UCLA and played together before turning pro. Poly's current brand of flashy football emerged from those elite athletes in the early 1980s, playing under Barnett, whose philosophy was to let players be themselves. Making the CIF title game three years in a row, even if they only won once, was a loud announcement that the Jackrabbits were back on the map and would have to be dealt with by anyone seeking the crown. Since 1980, the Jackrabbits have made the playoffs every single year, a streak of 32 after the 2011 season that set a new California record, according to *Cal Hi Sports' Almanac*.

Barnett's final two years failed to reach the heights of his first three, as Poly went 6–2–2 and 10–2, with a semifinal loss to Riverside Poly, its best effort. In that game, Mark Carrier was sidelined with an injury, which Barnett said was the difference. "They don't score 35 points on us if Carrier plays," Barnett said. He left for a number of reasons. For one, he didn't relish the idea of more community meetings. Barnett wanted to coach and be left alone, and the high-drama world of Poly football wasn't conducive to that. Leading up to the game against Compton in his final year, there was a death threat out on him. Barnett was asked by the police to wear a flack jacket, and he went in and out of the game with a police escort. On the way back to the bus, a Compton fan came running at them but was stopped by another officer. "That makes you think," Barnett said.

"When things were good at Poly, they were great. But when things were bad, they were *bad*. It can be a mess to sort out." Barnett managed to sort it out well enough to win a ring and officially reopen the championship era at Poly. He also put the pieces in place for his successor, a man who would push Poly to even greater heights.

A FOOTBALL FACTORY: JERRY JASO, 1985–2000

Jerry Jaso was a defensive back for the football team and a standout on the baseball team his junior and senior years at Poly in the late 1960s. He was an All-CIF baseball player on the 1968 team that won the Moore League title, the last time Poly would win it alone until 2012. Barnett had brought him back to his alma mater in 1980 as an assistant and, by the time he and co-head coach Thomas Whiting took over in 1985, he was ready to dig in. Jaso ran the defense and Whiting the offense.

After 1993, Whiting bowed out, but Jaso would remain for another huge championship push. His sixteen-year tenure in the head job is the longest in school history, and his four CIF title wins make him just one of three coaches to hit that plateau.

It's hard to imagine a splashier introduction to the Southern California football scene than the one Jaso made in 1985, his and Whiting's inaugural year. Poly's roster had boasted incredible talent before, but it's hard to argue against the credentials of the 1985 team, which featured not one but *two* young men—Mark Carrier and Leonard "Eight Ball" Russell—who would be named NFL Rookie of the Year. As would be the case for Poly in many of the coming championship years, most of the team's firepower was on defense, and the '85 team is perhaps the best defensive unit the school ever fielded. The team established a state record by giving up only a little more than five hundred rushing yards all season (just over forty-four yards per game, or eleven rushing yards per quarter for the whole season). The defense was led by Carrier, who went from Poly to USC, where he won the Jim Thorpe Award, an award given to the nation's top college defensive back. Carrier was not only the NFL's rookie of the year in 1990 but was also a three-time NFL Pro Bowler with the Bears as part of his decade-long career. He's been an NFL assistant coach since 2004, most recently with the Bengals. "There's a guy who completely maximized his potential," said Jaso. "And a born leader. He would get guys going in practice. He'd tell his teammates if they were sarcastic with them, 'I don't care what you think, you need to get your ass in gear.'"

The defense was strong up front and great in the linebacking corps and had a speedy, playmaking secondary. The players were physical and played a straight-up base defense with very little blitzing. They simply lined up and beat people.

Carrier's defense gave up just thirteen points in their first eight games and started the Moore League slate 4–0 by a combined score of 127–0. The Jackrabbits entered the regular season finale with Millikan ranked fourth in the country and were expected to roll right through to the playoffs. They had yet to yield a touchdown all season. But the Poly offense, which had sputtered at times, never got going, and the Jackrabbits didn't put the Rams away. They fell behind 9–0 but, in the fourth quarter, scored touchdowns on a pass from quarterback Mike Herring to Eric Morgan, and a nine-yard touchdown run by Russell, who had 203 yards on 29 carries that night. With 59 seconds left and a 13–9 lead, junior Lolo James recovered a fumble and set off a celebration on the Poly sidelines. The Jackrabbits looked safe.

But rather than run it or take a knee, Herring threw a pass—and Millikan's Bob Brown picked it off. With five seconds left on the clock, Rams quarterback Cliff Mosley hit Ed Robinson for a touchdown, giving Millikan an improbable 15–13 win.

After blowing out St. Paul 41–15 in the first round of the playoffs, Poly played the rest of the way to the championship on the edge of a razor, beating Fontana 10–9 and Marina 7–6. In the championship against the Edison Chargers, Poly trailed 14–0 halfway through the fourth quarter, with the clock ticking down awfully fast. Lineman Stacy Elliot made a huge play, reaching up for an interception and giving the offense the ball back. The Jackrabbits didn't waste any time; Russell scored three plays later.

Sensing that the Jackrabbits had the momentum, Edison went for it on fourth and one at Poly's forty-three on the next drive, trying to get the first down to run the clock out. But that year's defense was just too stout, and the team was walled up. With fifty-nine seconds left in the game, Herring hit Andre Hill to pull Poly within one. Not wanting to risk the miracle comeback, Poly's coaches decided to kick the extra point, taking a tie in the game and making the Jackrabbits co-champions.

It was a fitting way to end the year. The Jackrabbits were co-CIF champs and co-Moore League champs and they had co-captains who would be named the NFL's top rookies. Carrier was named co-CIF Player of the Year and, of course, the Jackrabbits were led that year by their first-ever co-head coaches, Jaso and Whiting.

Leonard Russell starred the next year as a senior. Awards came rolling in: Moore League Offensive Player of the Year, Gatorade California Player of the Year, All-CIF and more. Russell went on to play at Arizona State and was the first running back selected in the 1991 draft by the Patriots. That year, he gained over a thousand yards to lead all rookies, earning him top offensive rookie honors.

Poly cruised through the Moore League for the following seasons, not losing a game in between the 1982 defeat to Lakewood and a 1991 loss, but championship success didn't come. A parade of NFL talent continued to stream through the torn-up field at 1600 Atlantic, entering to learn from Jaso, Whiting and Poly's assistants and going forth to serve in the pro ranks. Willie McGinest, Marquez Pope, James Burton, Don Sasa, Omar Stoutmire

Willie McGinest was a terror on the football field, but he was also an All-State basketball player. *Poly yearbook.*

and Whiting's son, Brandon, all went pro in the 1990s, bolstering Poly's reputation as a talent powerhouse.

Each year, it seemed the team came up a little short, however. In 1988, Poly entered the playoffs 8–0–1, with fourteen returning starters off a team that had won a playoff game the year before. The Jackrabbits averaged 32.8 points per game and seemed headed for another title, but they were shocked by Crespi, 26–23, in the first round. In 1989, they won their tenth consecutive league title, but Willie McGinest's senior year was cut short by San Giorgino, 14–6, in the second round of the playoffs.

McGinest starred in both football and basketball, being named to the CIF All-State teams in both sports. As a linebacker at USC, McGinest was a three-time All-Pac 10 player and an All-American. He was then drafted fourth overall by the Patriots in 1994. While in New England, he won three Super Bowls, established an NFL postseason sack record that still stands and played in two NFL Pro Bowls. A charismatic television personality, he has done extensive work for the NFL Network since retiring and is one of several former Poly stars who can still be seen frequenting the sidelines regularly at Vets.

Marquez Pope was one in a long line of star safeties on the late 1980s teams, going to Fresno State out of Poly and then going on to a successful ten-year NFL career. He is thought to be the only Jackrabbit with an NFL rule named after him (the Marquez Pope Rule, which states that a fumble recovered by a defensive player will be spotted at the spot of the recovery, not where the player's momentum leads him), which was enacted after he had a recovered fumble that was ruled a safety. He is also the only player in NFL history to play for all four California teams—the San Diego Chargers (which drafted him), the LA Rams, the San Francisco 49ers and the Oakland Raiders.

Starring in the early 1990s was Brandon Whiting, son of co-head coach Thomas. Although his father was an offensive coach, Brandon won his acclaim as a powerhouse defensive lineman, earning Moore League Defensive Player of the Year honors. Whiting was also an excellent student and went on to start for four years at UC Berkeley (Cal), where he excelled, and he was drafted by the Eagles in 1998. He played there for six seasons before being traded to the 49ers for receiver Terrell Owens.

But while the players were great, the team was languishing in the first few rounds of the playoffs. In 1991, the team had its first losing record since 1973, going 5–6 (but still 4–1 in a weakening Moore League). It regained its footing after that, but it was still losing second-round games to Fontana, Mater Dei and Los Alamitos. Whiting left after his son graduated following the 1993 season. The next year, 1994, was mostly notable for a 28–0 skunking by Jordan—it was the last time Poly would lose to a Moore League opponent until 2009, a span of eighty games that still stands as a California record. Impatient Poly fans didn't have long to wait, however. The era of unparalleled dominance was upon them.

The Ring's The Thing

Most historic high school powers fade. Either new, richer schools pop up in their area, or they close. Or, sometimes, there is some other shift in athletic demographics that dulls their brightness. At Poly, for whatever reason, things have only gotten better. Jaso took the 1995 and '96 Jackrabbits to the semifinals, the opening shots in a remarkable run. From 1995 to 2008, the team failed to make semifinals in CIF's highest division just once. In those fourteen seasons, it played in nine championship games and won seven of the school's eighteen titles. That so many of Poly's CIF banners were hung in an era when the team was being outspent by the emerging rich, private Catholic schools makes the number that much more impressive. Over the final four years Jaso was head coach, the team went 54–1–1 and won three CIF titles.

"What Jerry took the time to do," said Bob Keisser, a *Press-Telegram* columnist and Long Beach sports historian, "was to really tap back into the history of the school. When I walked into the locker room for the first time, he had all these photos of all the great players. They were in his office, down the hallway, in the film room. He was selling the history of the program. I don't know of many high schools that do that."

In 1995, the team started 12–0 and looked destined to reach that level. Akka-Ar Moses and Ken-Yon Rambo led the offense (Rambo played in the NFL for five years before moving to the Canadian Football League, where he is still active), while Joe Harris took the Moore League's Defensive Player of the Year honors. But after beating Edison and Capistrano Valley in the playoffs, the Jackrabbits, ranked number two, ran up against Bishop Amat in the semifinals and lost 28–27, when they decided to go for two and didn't get it.

In 1996, the team again fell in the semifinals, this time to another Catholic school, Mater Dei. While Rambo was fantastic as a senior, it was the sophomore class that had people talking. Quarterback Chris Lewis was tall, bright and accurate, and his good friend Darrell Rideaux was a diminutive, shockingly fast defensive back. They and the rest of the Jackrabbits' sophomore class (which featured an astounding five future pro players) vowed to see the Mater Dei Monarchs again the next year. And they would.

You can't talk about the next years of Poly history or, at least, fully understand it, without first talking about Mater Dei. A private school located in the heart of Orange County, in Santa Ana, the Monarchs are the definition of a Catholic power. So when these teams met three times over the next three seasons, it understandably felt like there was more at stake than just a CIF title. The fact that they met in the championship three times in a row is remarkable in and of itself—that's never happened before or since in the CIF's highest division.

"I kind of equate it to Republicans and Democrats," said Keisser. "Mater Dei, the Republicans, love their team, right or wrong. They defend their team, and they're always behind [head coach] Bruce Rollinson. Poly is liberal, they take chances. They can be critical of each other at times. And of course, they're an urban school—the ultimate urban school."

The differences were highlighted at the prechampionship walk through with CIF officials and the head coaches, Jaso and Mater Dei's Bruce Rollinson. Poly's Joe Carlson was there as a young, inexperienced athletic director and recalled, "Just watching them and their ability to maneuver everything for themselves. The CIF would say, 'Oh yes, here's your doctor's pass,' and they'd say, 'Oh we have four doctors.' And then we'd say, 'Uh, so do we!' Any time they said something we just went, 'Us too!'"

Carlson also remembered Rollinson talking about playing with USC in the Coliseum and, how the last time he was there, USC was playing UCLA. Jaso smiled to himself and later told Carlson, "He's talking about a game I played in (for UCLA). I actually intercepted a pass, and we beat USC that day."

"That's who Jerry is," said Carlson. "He didn't get in Rollinson's face or show him up, he just savored the joke and kept it to himself."

The year 1997 was supposed to be Mater Dei's year. But with Lewis spreading the ball around at an unheard-of clip for a Poly quarterback, Herman Ho-Ching pounding the rock and an athletic, playmaking defense, Poly had something to say about it. By the time the team entered the playoffs, it was like a sharpened blade, having gone 10–0 in the regular season with wins over Carson, Banning and Dominguez. The Jackrabbits beat

Dominguez 28–13, the closest regular season game they had. The Moore League was barely a tackling dummy at that point, and Poly went 5–0 by a combined 270–37 (an average score of 54–7).

In the playoffs that year, everyone was just waiting for the Jackrabbits and Monarchs to meet in the championship. Poly dispatched Fountain Valley, Redlands and Loyola (which hadn't lost a game thus far, either), to set up the long-awaited championship, which was played at the Coliseum.

The Monarchs took a 17–7 lead, but the Jackrabbits didn't give up. Lewis hit Ho-Ching for touchdowns of 66 and 32 yards, and the running back's third touchdown of the night put Poly ahead, which is where it would end the game and the season. The win snapped Mater Dei's twenty-seven-game win streak and gave Poly its first CIF rings since 1985. In addition to his three scores, the heroic Ho-Ching had another 90-plus-yard score called back on a penalty. Lewis was 11 for 16 for 264 yards, with three of those incompletions two-handed drops.

Jaso and Carlson both wryly recalled that Mater Dei had a large balloon arch in the west end zone. After Poly won, some of the Poly players went and began popping the balloons. Mater Dei was so incensed that it sent Poly a bill for several hundred dollars. "That was the start of some of the...let's say, 'flavor' of that rivalry," said Carlson.

Keisser remembered it, too. "This was my first real Mater Dei experience," he said. "When the Poly kids were popping them, the Mater Dei fans and officials in the press box said, 'Tsk tsk, why are they doing that?,' calling them hoodlums. I said, 'But did you really need a forty-yard-long balloon display? Was it *really* necessary?'"

The sense of history sprung back to life, like water returning to a dry riverbed, and it was everywhere. Jaso told Keisser: "When a kid comes to Poly, he is reminded from the beginning about all of the great kids who played here and went on to college and the pros. You don't win fourteen games a year just on talent. Tradition is a big part of our success. The kids know what it is to be Poly."

The next year, however, proved frustrating. In his senior season, Lewis broke every major California passing record, finishing with a state record of 107 touchdowns. That mark was made all the more impressive by the fact that the future Stanford player barely played at all in the second half of Moore League games. Lewis was named an All-American and was Gatorade's State Player of the Year. He went on to star in NFL Europe and to have a short stint with the Arizona Cardinals. His supporting cast was unreal as well—Kareem Kelly and Samie Parker were his wideouts, a pair

Darrell Rideaux (left) trains with Kawika Watts on the Poly track team after the football team's 1997 title win. The diminutive corner's speed allowed him to take chances others couldn't. *Poly yearbook.*

of studs who went on to successful careers at USC and Oregon and then on to the pros. The running back was Larry Croom, who would go pro as well, as would cornerback Darrell Rideaux (who anchored the defense while also winning state championships in track as California's fastest high school student). Parker set a Poly single-season record at the school with 1,200 yards and 19 touchdowns.

So it wasn't just modesty when Lewis said, "It's an unbelievable feeling to know that my name is going to be at the top of record books—but it would not have been possible without the surrounding cast: linemen, receivers, and the rest of my team."

Jaso appreciated the luxury that a bright quarterback gave him and, fifteen years later, he still remembered mid-game adjustments the two of them put in. There were also more instinctual plays. "We played Amat in the semis [in 1998], and they had a corner who for some reason got up in the face of Kareem Kelly," Jaso said. "And I just yelled, 'Chris!' as loud as I could. And he just looked and gave me a, 'Yeah I got this' face. And then he bombed it to Kareem, easy touchdown. We go up by two touchdowns in the fourth quarter, and you just weren't going to catch us with a lead like that."

In 1998, the Moore League was once again brushed aside with all the care a truck gives a fly that hits its windshield, as Poly outscored its league opponents 302–26 (an average score of 60–5), despite not playing its starters in the second half. This time, the team blew through the playoffs in similar fashion, dropping Huntington Beach by 52, Loyola by 15 and Bishop Amat by 26. That set up the game everyone had been waiting for: Jackrabbits v. Monarchs, round two. This time it was Poly that was favored to win. But once again, it was time for an upset for the CIF's top team.

Matt Grootegoed, who would go on to USC with Rideaux and Kelly, gave an almost inhuman performance against the Jackrabbits that led his team to a 33–26 victory. He carried the ball thirty-three times for 244 yards and two touchdowns. On defense, he had seven tackles and two pass deflections. "It was a super-heroic effort," said Rob Shock, Poly's current athletic director.

"That was a disappointing game," said Jaso. "We didn't put our best foot forward that night."

The season ended in disappointment for the ultra-talented Jackrabbits, who had set a school record with 645 points scored. And with ten players signing Divison 1 scholarships (tying their own state record), five of whom would play professionally, concerns were already raised about how Poly could rebuild with so much talent leaving.

It was around this time that people began saying: "Poly doesn't rebuild. They reload."

The sophomores who would step into the big cleats vacated by the last year's senior class would become, arguably, the greatest class of high school football players ever produced, anywhere. In the next three years, the Jackrabbits would win three straight CIF championships, a record no other team has touched and one that would extend Poly's streak to five consecutive CIF title game appearances, also something that's never been done.

The extension of dominance was keyed by the ascendance of the Fab Five (or the Big Five)—five players who were so good that different national publications actually had different names by which to refer to them. Hershel Dennis (running back), Marcedes Lewis (tight end, defensive end), Manuel Wright (defensive tackle), Winston Justice (offensive tackle) and Darnell Bing (safety) were all rated among the best three players at their position in the country. In their senior season, all five were named PARADE All-Americans, the only time five players at one school have earned that honor. That this was happening at Long Beach Poly, where players practiced on a muddy square of grass also used by the school's baseball and soccer teams, baffled national pundits.

The Fab Five wasted no time letting people think about how good they would or could be in their sophomore seasons, however. They went right after it, winning close games in a tough nonleague schedule, before waving goodbye to the Moore League competition. When the playoffs came around and the brackets were released on a warm Southern California Sunday, all eyes turned to Poly and Mater Dei, which were on opposite sides of the sheet. Could the area's best public and private school really pull off a third straight championship game, a rubber match, to decide the decade's best school?

Well, they could. And sure enough, on December 12, once again at Edison Field in Anaheim before a monster crowd of 19,000, the two teams met in the championship. Poly's win two years prior had ended Mater Dei's twenty-seven-game streak, and Mater Dei's win in 1998 ended Poly's twenty-seven-game winning streak. It was to be the ultimate deciding contest. However, nothing would be decided.

Grootegoed left the game early in the first quarter after spraining his ankle, preventing him from duplicating his monster performance of the previous season. Poly scored a flurry of touchdowns in the second quarter, as quarterback Brandon Fasavalu threw for a pair of touchdowns, and Dennis's 79-yard run was followed by a Douglas Hines plunge. (Dennis finished with 144 yards). Poly led 21–10, but the Matt Leinert-led Monarchs marched back and tied the game at 21 in the third quarter. That was all the scoring that would happen that day.

Poly was driving in the two-minute drill when a pass to Marcedes Lewis moved the Jackrabbits across midfield, but the play was called back for an illegal procedure penalty. "If we get that, we're gonna go down and score," said Jaso. Poly punted instead and, after a Hail Mary attempt that Poly almost picked off, Rollinson decided to kneel the ball. The game ended in a tie, 21–21.

"It's not really as satisfying," said Jaso. "It's a funky deal."

"It's a big letdown," Dennis said at the time. "We worked hard all week. We didn't work hard just to be co-champs."

Still, looking back on that three-year series, which the teams split with one win, one loss and one tie apiece, it's pretty remarkable. "Our budget at Poly was around $5,000 a year," said Jaso. "I heard Mater Dei's was close to $250,000. So in those years we were even, it was $15,000 against $750,000, and they didn't get us. It was fun beating them, there's no question about that. And I think it was great for the school, too."

With the Fab Five, the hard-hitting linebacker Marvin Simmons and defensive end Ray Tago all returning the next year, the Jackrabbits were primed for a repeat. Many fans and players were as unhappy about the tie as Poly students had been about the 1910 league title tie. But there was no doubt that Poly was the favorite to take it home in 2000, continuing its historic run.

Dennis would take over the Poly rushing record from Kirk Jones, a record that has been passed down from Poly great to Poly great. Drawing a ton of national attention, the 2000 team conquered the competition, winning every game it played. It beat Vista, Banning, Santa Barbara, Fontana and Dominguez in the preseason by a combined score of 192–35 and then swept the Moore League aside once again, outscoring opponents 223–27. The playoffs didn't post much resistance, either, as Poly beat Fountain Valley by 24, St. Paul by 21 and Esperanza by 21 to get to the championship.

Once again, Poly would meet a moneyed private school, and cultures would clash between the hash marks. But this time, Mater Dei wasn't prepared to keep its championship appointment with Poly, and Loyola would have to stand in. The storylines were the same—the "athletic" Jackrabbits prepared to meet the "disciplined" Cubs before 12,000 in Anaheim.

The Cubs pulled off a trick play, utilizing the fumblerooski for a forty-two-yard gain, which imperiled the Jackrabbits' chances. That set up a touchdown pass that gave Loyola a 10–7 lead with just over a minute remaining. But while some fans had wondered if the blowout-happy Jackrabbits would be battle-tested for a close championship, Jaso's group was ready. Poly marched downfield and kicker Javier Torres (who had missed a thirty-four yard attempt earlier) drilled a field goal with four seconds left to tie the game at the end of regulation. Unlike the 1999 game with Mater

Hershel Dennis in action in 2000. The running back was a nearly unstoppable blend of elusive speed and explosive power. *Poly yearbook.*

Dei, there would be no tie. Poly had pushed the CIF hard to change that rule and, sure enough, in the first year that overtime had been enacted, the Jackrabbits got to test it out.

The system was based on alternating possessions, giving each team a chance to score, like the NCAA. The Cubs kicked a field goal on their possession, after driving to the four but failing to score. Poly moved down to the eleven yard line, and quarterback Brandon Brooks got the ball to Dennis, who made a Cub player miss. He scampered into the end zone, giving Poly a 16–13 victory.

According to Rob Shock, a trainer with the team at the time, Dennis's performance that postseason was even more impressive than most knew.

"He had a broken rib," said Shock. "He was cleared, but it hurt him like Hell. He just kept taking treatments, trying to wrap it, and going out there and running in incredible pain."

The Dick Butkus Football Network declared Poly the national champions after its 14–0 tour de force season, its fourth time ever winning every game played in a season, and its second time under Jaso. People were already entertaining thoughts of 2001 and the possibility of the CIF's first-ever three-peat. With the Fab Five returning, Jaso at the helm and the Poly football factory firing on all cylinders, it didn't seem that anything could throw the Jackrabbits off track.

Poly: The Nation's Best

Whether the football team's success was a part of the renaissance happening at Poly or whether that renaissance was keyed by football, there was no denying how far Poly had come by the 1990s. By the end of the decade, the school was leading the nation in acceptances to UCLA and Berkeley, thanks to the PACE and CIC magnets. Poly also had more students accepted to Ivy League schools in that time than any other public school in the country.

It was hard to believe that just a few decades before, the campus was almost shut down. Shawn Ashley, who was a student during the race fights of 1970 and then co-principal from 1996–2011, was there for a lot of that turnaround, which was also keyed by Carl Cohn's time as principal and superintendent.

"It's interesting, the history of schools that have race riots is that within about three years, they typically flip over to being all minority," said Ashley. "Typically there's white flight and they abandon the school. But that didn't happen at Poly, because people wanted to send their kids here, and programs like PACE and CIC were created to help that happen."

There was also a fighting spirit perfectly represented by Ashley himself. After getting sucker-punched by a fellow student while trying to stop a fight from happening in 1970, Ashley was taken to the hospital to receive nine stitches. "I was back at school the next day," he said. "I wasn't a quitter."

Neither was his school. Thanks to programs like the academic magnets and the music department, Poly came back better and stronger than before.

Sports Illustrated named Long Beach Poly the top athletic program in the nation. *Poly archives.*

"And then, at some point, all this diversity goes from being a problem to being a strength," said Ashley. "And actually, when Poly beat Mater Dei in 1997, that in my opinion was what spring-boarded the school. That got us a front-page story on the *Los Angeles Times*, and it seemed like from that moment, the momentum just caught. I give that victory a lot of credit for the great stuff that happened the next fifteen years while I was there. A good football team makes a world of difference."

The school won CIF championships in seemingly every sport, winning the CIF Commissioner's Cup in 1998–99, 1999–2000 and 2001–02. From 1991–2010, only one other public school won the award, and it was tony Paso Robles High School. While the school was undergoing an academic and athletic revitalization, it also reestablished its record as a place where many races and cultures coexisted harmoniously. Even the musicians got into it; Poly won three consecutive Grammy awards for having the best overall music program of any school in the nation.

The school was living in a peaceful bubble, represented well by a juggernaut football program. But then, in late May, Jerry Jaso shocked the Poly world, announcing that he was leaving the school for a job at Long Beach City College.

New World, Same Poly: Raul Lara, 2001–Present

You would have thought the sky was falling down on top of Long Beach. Speculation in the city's barbershops ran from the insulting (Jaso was being forced out for one of a number of different offenses) to the absurd (he was leaving because he was afraid of losing a marquee game that year). Everyone had his or her own opinion—and legitimately, for the timing was strange. The greatest class of players to ever come out of the school was just months from their senior season and, looming ahead, they were to play De La Salle in October in the first-ever high school national championship game.

Jaso said the decision was much easier and less interesting than any of the rumors made it out to be. "Look, first, Barnett left us a championship team, and he knew it—I was happy to do the same. I was topped out, salary-wise, in the district, and at City College I got a raise. I had two kids going to college—it was a good deal. And I loved Poly, but I was there coaching twenty-one years, and I was a student for three years, so when I left I'd been there half my life."

A hasty search for a new coach drew two names: Kirk Jones, the former star running back, and Raul Lara, Jaso's defensive coordinator. There was, once again, a rift in the community. Many black Poly supporters wanted to see Jones become the first black coach to be named sole coach of the team. Any sense of rivalry flew over the heads of Jones and Lara, who met in Lara's office and struck a deal: if Lara got the job, Jones would be his offensive coordinator. If Jones got the job, Lara would be his defensive coordinator.

The next morning, Lara got a phone call: Jones had died of a massive heart attack. The job was his, but he had lost a friend, the team had lost a

The 2001 Poly team, perhaps the most talented high school team in history, with six future NFL players and twenty-eight Division 1 signees. *Poly yearbook.*

coach and the players and community had lost a father figure and dear friend. Whatever was to come in 2001, it would be done in Kirk Jones's name.

What was to come, of course, was the media circus of all media circuses. The game against De La Salle, ranked number two in the nation to Poly's number one, was circled on every calendar in the city. It was to be the first time the top two teams in the nation met to decide a true national champion, an occasion so momentous that Poly alum Don Wallace wrote a book about it, *One Great Game*.

"I'll never forget watching their film for the first time," said Lara. "I popped it in and I'm like, 'Oh my God, what did Jerry get me into?' I've never even seen a college team get off the ball like that."

Everything prior to the game felt like foreplay. The Jackrabbits dispatched Westchester 37–0. Their second game was canceled following the tragedy of September 11. The Jackrabbits resumed action to defeat Narbonne 28–6 and Fontana 70–0, setting up the clash between Poly and De La Salle.

The De La Salle Spartans came from posh, lily-white Concord to challenge Poly. De La Salle hadn't lost since 1992 but hadn't played a group of athletes like Poly's 2001 team (though it's worth noting that the Fab Five were the core of arguably the greatest group of talent on a high school team,

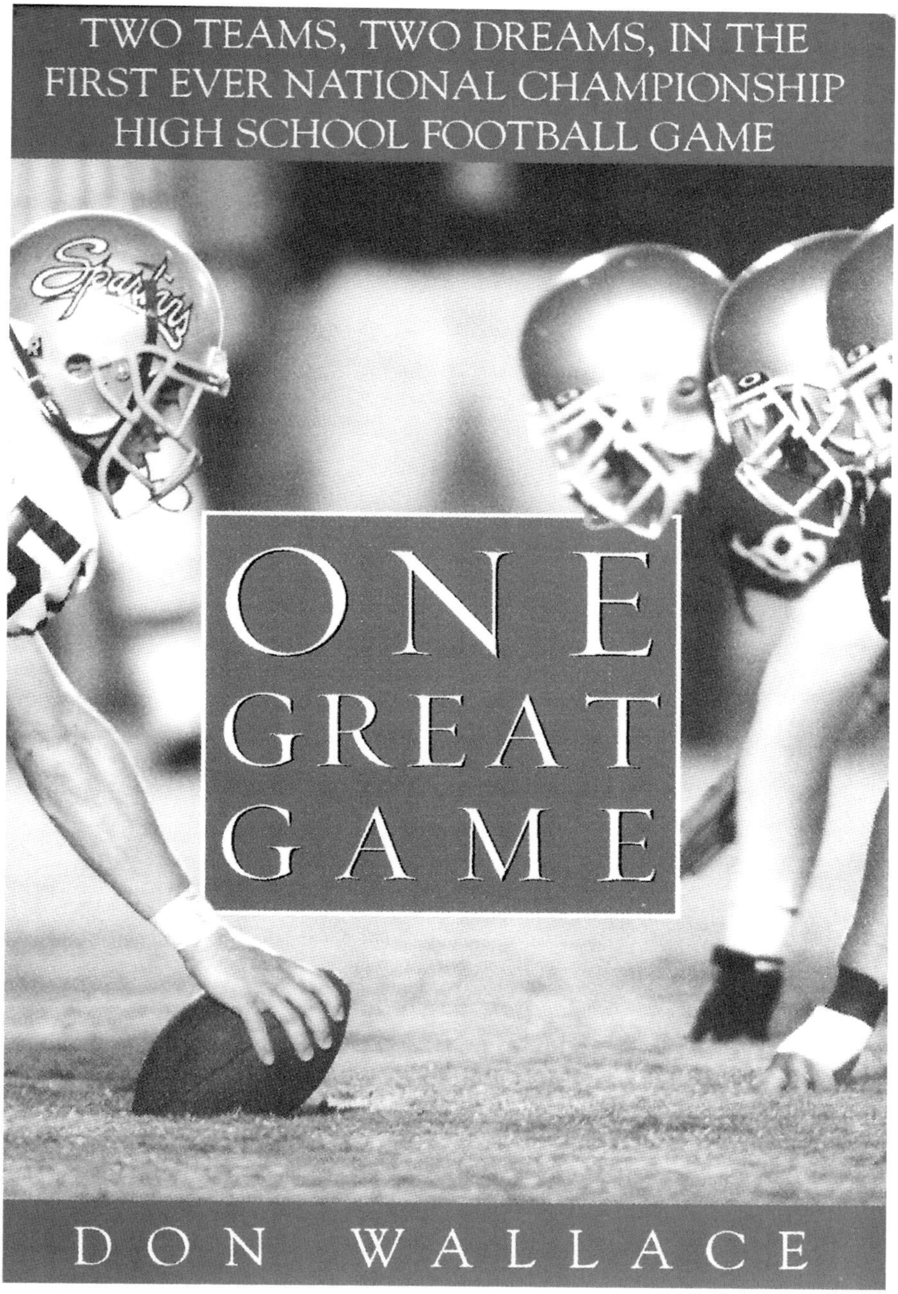

Cover of *One Great Game*, a book written by Don Wallace about the 2001 national championship game between Poly and De La Salle. *Photo by the author.*

so perhaps nobody had). Athletic director Joe Carlson and principals Shawn Ashley and Mel Collins set about preparing for the game like a Division 1 NCAA athletic department. "We had to put stands on the other side of Vets, get a professional ticket maker, sell tickets through the mail, all that stuff," said Carlson. "And we had to do a lot for De La Salle, in terms of travel and food—there was no backing down from that, they wanted a lot."

The buildup was incredible, with a parade, rallies—even a brief showing of moral support from some of the other schools. Millikan had a "Good luck Poly" sign up, and businesses all over town had similar messages in their windows.

The game drew over 17,000 fans to Vets, despite the fact that the game was televised nationally (a first for a high school game) and that scalpers were hocking the sold-out tickets for upwards of $100 at the door. The noise was so huge that the stadium simultaneously felt like it was an NFL stadium and a small backyard lot. Over forty players were on the field, and all would become Division 1 signees; nine would be NFL players. It was Raul Lara's fourth game as head coach.

The Spartans had just three starters back, while Poly had five All-Americans and six of *Sports Illustrated*'s top 100. Wallace had helped make sure all of the potentially interested media across the country was informed about the game, and they showed up in force. *Sports Illustrated* reportedly had a cover ready to run if Poly had won the game. But Maurice Drew (who would play with Marcedes Lewis at UCLA and for the Jacksonville Jaguars as Maurice Jones-Drew) torched Poly for 165 yards and 4 TDs. There was some trickery by the De La Salle coaches, who had only played Drew at safety all year and then moved him to running back for the first time against Poly. "They jobbed us pretty good with that one," said Carlson.

With all that talent, the game was played on another level. Wallace was standing on the Poly sideline next to Mark Carrier, who remarked to him, "I've never seen this type of speed in a high school game."

"All us old guys probably had our pulses running around 160," said Wallace.

The whole stadium's heart rate spiked when Poly almost scored on its first offensive play. Lara went for the home run, and Brooks threw a rocket for freshman Derrick Jones, who dropped a ball that would have been a long touchdown. De La Salle would go up 14–3, but Marcedes Lewis's twelve-yard touchdown catch from Brooks made it 21–15 Spartans at halftime. But Drew scored again in the second half to seal a 28–15 victory that gave the Spartans the national title, and the Jackrabbits a bad case of heartburn.

Program cover from the 2001 national championship game between Poly and De La Salle. *Courtesy David Hendrickson.*

Years later, the dropped pass still haunts some members of the Poly staff. Current Poly athletic director Rob Shock, who was the trainer then, still thinks of it often. Before the game, Jones had asked him to put an Oakley visor on his helmet. Since it was a nationally televised game, and Oakley was a sponsor, Shock happily took the face mask off of Jones's helmet and clamped the visor into place. "He'd never practiced with one, never played with one," said Shock, shaking his head. "I don't know if it's my fault or not. But I know he later said he lost the ball in the glare, and I know right after that series he asked me to take the visor out. First thing he did, coming off the field. That's one that sits in my head, it plays in my head. If he gets that catch, we go up, that's a different game. I've never asked him if that visor was responsible, because I don't want to know if it's true or not. But now, I'd definitely have him practice in it if he was going to wear it."

"You know, that was one of the most composed, competitive big games I ever saw Poly play," said Jim McCormick, who covered Long Beach sports for the *Press-Telegram* from 1960–2006, "And I was impressed with them, because they never stopped trying to do what they needed to do to win—they just couldn't quite pull it off."

"If I was to rewind time over," said Lara, looking like he wishes he could, "Hershel (Dennis) would have run the ball a lot more. And Marcedes would have been a bigger part of the plan. That one eats me up." Despite a career as successful as anyone else's at Poly in terms of CIF rings and winning percentage, Lara has, at times, faced criticism from Poly fans. When asked if he thought winning that game would have changed the way people saw him, he didn't hesitate: "Yeah. Oh yeah."

Fortunately for the Jackrabbits, the Moore League started the next week, and they could beat up on their league-mates. They went 5–0 again, outscoring their opponents 277–44. In the playoffs, they beat Fountain Valley by 38, Loyola by 8 and Los Alamitos by 21. That set up a championship game against Huntington Beach Edison; the Jackrabbits decided to spare their fans the suspense, more than redeeming their season with a 42–28 win that made them the first three-peat champions in CIF history.

When the season ended, the world of high school sports was forever altered. America had begun to transition into a nation where contracts to televise high school sports were million-dollar deals and where recruiting sites followed athletes around relentlessly, hoping for nuggets of info about college commitments like dropped crumbs. Through that increasing maelstrom of media, Lara has been a steady hand. Part of that is his "day job," which is actually the graveyard shift as a probation officer for Los Angeles County.

After a few of the championships his teams won, Lara got in his car and went to work, not getting to sleep until early the next morning. Lara has long said that, with his occupation, it's easy to keep things in perspective.

It's been easy to keep a perspective on that year's senior class, too. Lewis has been the most visible, winning the John Mackey Award at UCLA as the nation's top NCAA tight end. He's gone on to a long, NFL Pro Bowl career with the Jacksonville Jaguars, while continuing a relationship with Poly that's included significant financial support. The other four members of the Fab Five all went to USC. Justice has had a long NFL career as well. Knee problems, meanwhile, derailed Dennis's career, who finished at Poly with 5,362 yards and 83 touchdowns.

Bing and Wright both made the NFL, too, and even Dennis was able to make the most of his injury, becoming the first player in Pac-10 history to be on six conference championship teams. He is also the all-time winningest player in NCAA history, thanks to six years as a Trojan in that school's heyday.

With so much talent graduating, it's no wonder that it took the Jackrabbits a few years to get their feet back under them. They beat Hawaii state champ Kahuku the next year, lost a rematch with De La Salle and ended their 2002 season in the semifinals in a 21–20 heartbreaker, especially as Poly had led 20–7 in the third quarter. It was the first time since 1996 that Poly hadn't made the championship. But the team's absence wasn't an extended one, as it would return each of the next two years.

In 2003, the Jackrabbits had probably the fastest wide receiver duo in high school history, with Jones in his senior year and DeSean Jackson blazing the sidelines too. Both were sub-4.4 40 athletes, and William Alo (the school's all-time leading tackler) anchored a defense that made sure the Jackrabbits wouldn't need to score many points to win games. Poly beat Mater Dei in the semifinals that year to get back to the championship, but Loyola handed the team a 21–17 loss (Poly had led 14–0 but once again gave up the lead).

The next year, the Jackrabbits lost a nonleague game to Mission Viejo but otherwise wouldn't be denied, fitting for a year that featured Alo and DeSean "Action" Jackson, as thrilling and dynamic a player as any high school field had ever seen. Poly won every playoff game that year by at least three touchdowns, setting up another Angel Stadium championship, this time against Los Alamitos, an Orange County public school located just a few miles east of Long Beach.

Poly went up 7–0 after an incredible interception and sixty-eight yard touchdown return by Jackson, but the Griffins would answer, scoring but

DeSean "Action" Jackson making an extraordinary catch in 2003. *Poly yearbook.*

missing the extra point to pull within one, 7–6, with just under ten minutes left in the game. Running back Troy Guthrie keyed a seventy-five-yard drive, capped by quarterback Theodisthree Scott's keeper touchdown. They scored an insurance touchdown later to seal the 21–6 win, as Jackson finished with a pair of interceptions.

The next year was a ground-up rebuilding as the Jackrabbits lost three games and failed to make the semis for the first time since 1994. Those hoping for the demise of Poly, however, were sorely disappointed. In 2006, the team made its way back into the semis, beating Mater Dei in a thick fog at Vets Stadium and Sherman Oaks Notre Dame before meeting Orange Lutheran, another Catholic power, in the semifinals.

The Jackrabbits trailed 23–0 with seven minutes left in the game but came roaring back, overcoming some strange officiating decisions to bring the score to 23–22. But a botched snap and hold on the extra point cost them the chance to tie the game and force overtime. The next year's teams would be remembered not just for winning but for how close they were. Both Lara and defensive coordinator Jeff Turley brought up their off-field bond when asked about the teams, and linebacker George Daily-Lyles agreed. "There was always something to be done as a group of guys," he said. "No matter if it was five, or ten, we were always together, getting burgers at Tomy's or just hanging out in the film room. That translated well to the field."

In 2007, the Jackrabbits would not only win their seventeenth CIF championship and get their revenge on Orange Lutheran—they would also end up putting on the greatest single-game defensive performance in CIF history. They opened the season with a win over a team in Ohio and then a costly loss to Los Angeles power Birmingham. In the playoffs, they beat

Members of the 2005 Poly defense, including Kenny Rowe and Vaughn Telemaque. *Poly yearbook.*

Santa Margarita and Newport Harbor (for the second time that season), setting up a semifinal rematch with O. Lu.

Poly took a 2–0 lead when an Orange Lutheran snap on a punt went awry, scoring a safety. Lara remembered saying into his microphone, "We might just win this game 2–0 the way our defense is playing." That young unit, made up mostly of juniors, would in fact play absolutely lights out. The team had a goal-line stand at the end of the first half and went the whole game without giving up a score. But still, O. Lu had the ball with less than thirty seconds left, and a Poly offsides call put the ball just inches away from the end zone. The Lancers had a reliable kicker and figured if they didn't get the touchdown on second down that they could just boot it in and win by the preposterous score of 3–2.

"Coach Lara called a timeout," remembered George Daily-Lyles, a linebacker on that team and California State Player of the Year in 2008. "Instead of talking to us, he just let us get our heads right. And we walked out there, calm, like, 'We got this.'"

Instead of the Lancers scoring or centering the ball for their field goal kicker, the ball popped out on the handoff and bounced between Daily-Lyles's legs and Poly's Herman Davidson dove on it. Poly's ball! Two kneel-downs later, and Poly was headed to the championship thanks to a 2–0 win, which even many of the oldest Poly fans in attendance said was the most remarkable game they had ever seen. In fact, Lara had a series of photos of the final play blown up and posted in the Poly film room, where they remain, with the words "Never never never never never never...give up!" underneath.

"I love those things," laughed Daily-Lyles. "I'm forever immortalized at Long Beach Poly. They teach so much about the history, it's ingrained in you—being a part of that is amazing."

"As a defensive coordinator," Jeff Turley said, "a 2–0 game...you can't say much more than that. Damn."

After that game, the championship against Crespi seemed almost anticlimactic; Poly won 13–3. Star running back Melvin Richardson had two touchdowns on 157 yards of production. The defense held its opponent out of the end zone for the second consecutive game, having given up just 24 points in four playoff contests. What was so exciting for Lara and defensive coordinator Jeff Turley was that, with the exception of Jurrell Casey (currently with the Tennessee Titans) and Vaughn Telemaque (who went on to star at the University of Miami), the entire defense was coming back the next year, along with several key starters on offense. The year ended in disappointment. Poly wasn't selected for one of the newly founded State Bowl games, thanks to that early-season loss to Birmingham. That made the team even more determined to come back in 2008 and take care of business. The Jackrabbits opened what would end up being their fifth successful title defense with a long road trip, beating Miami Northwestern on the road in Florida, 29–7—just the third time in history a California team had beaten a Florida squad. They beat Newport Harbor and Carson and had a narrow 12–7 win over St. Bonaventure. Then they swept through the league, this time without a blemish on their record. If they could win another championship, they would be into the State Bowl.

But the road there was rocky and filled with nail-biters. In the first round, they beat Bishop Amat by coming from behind in the fourth quarter, beating the Lancers 21–17. Against Esperanza in the second round, Poly led 10–0 at halftime, but the Aztecs came back and tied it at 10, before the Jackrabbits got a huge gain on a tackle-eligible pass from quarterback Morgan Fennell to Julian Camper, setting up Richardson's game-winning plunge.

The semifinal game was a banner day for the Moore League, as Poly and Lakewood met at Cerritos College before a sold-out crowd of over 12,000 people. Even though it wasn't for a championship (and Poly had already beaten Lakewood earlier that year for another league crown), it felt like the biggest non-championship game since the De La Salle contest in 2001. Lakewood led 10–3 at halftime, but Poly scored 17 unanswered in the second half to take the win and the title berth. There, the team met Tesoro in another game that won't soon be forgotten, trailing 14–7 after three quarters but storming back to win it 20–17 after one of the most thrilling plays in CIF title game history.

Poly actually fell behind 17–7 with under ten minutes remaining, but Fennell hit Damon Smith for a ballsy twenty-four yard touchdown on fourth down. Then, with under three minutes remaining, Fennell handed off to Richardson, and the beefy running back plowed—absolutely crushed—Tesoro linebacker and Orange County Player of the Year Preston King. Richardson sprung free to the right sideline and ripped off to the end zone, winning Poly the school's eighteenth CIF championship.

It was a wonderful accomplishment for a group generally acknowledged as not being the most talented in recent Poly history, but noted for having perhaps the most heart and the most love for each other as teammates and brothers. None more so than the State Player of the Year, linebacker George Daily-Lyles, and the scat-back running back, Daveon Barner—who were actually brothers.

That Poly team earned the right to play for a state title, but fans' hopes that it would be a Poly/De La Salle rematch were crushed by the CIF State organization, which picked a little-known team from Sacramento named Grant. The Pacers looked, well, a lot like Poly. They were a big, fast inner-city team with Pacific Islanders and an underdog mentality. Grant fans streamed down Interstate-5 for the game, played at the Home Depot Center in Carson.

Grant would end up beating Poly 25–20. The Jackrabbits' running game couldn't get going, and the Pacers wore them down. It was a sad end for Daily-Lyles and his defense (he finished just one tackle shy of the school's all-time tackle record), but a championship season nonetheless. Daily-Lyles provided insight into the high level of expectations at the school five years later, saying, "That game still hurts. There's not a day that's gone by where I haven't thought about it. It tears at me—I hate that game. If we'd won, I think I'd wear my rings a little more. They're in a box somewhere in my garage. The loss definitely outweighs the wins."

It's a statement that is almost shocking but also almost expected at Poly, where expectations usually border on the ludicrous. When Jaso or Lara were asked about their fans' expectations for the team, both rolled their eyes. Rob Shock compared it to working with the Lakers, as opposed to an underfunded inner-city high school.

It's led to strange circumstances like Lara, who has won four CIF titles, being badmouthed in the Vets stands so much that Bob Keisser wrote a

Brothers Daveon Barner and George Daily-Lyles (California State's player of the year) praying before the state championship against Grant in 2008. *Poly yearbook.*

newspaper column about it. "There was a time when Jaso and Whiting were head coaches that a petition circulated to get *them* fired," said Lara. Since his retirement, Jaso has been viewed more with rosy lenses, a fate perhaps in store for Lara, too, with his four CIF titles. For now, despite being among the most successful coaches in school history, it's relentless. "I'm a Poly guy, so I understand the expectation thing," said Lara. "If I was sitting up there, I'd probably be criticizing me sometimes, too."

"Let's just say it's more fun to get there than to stay there, alright?" said Jaso, who admitted he was just fine with getting away from that aspect of coaching at Poly. He said longtime Poly community fixture Erroll Parker walked into a bar on a night Poly had beaten Lakewood 72–7 in the late 1990s, and there were a bunch of Poly alums sitting around, cussing about what an idiot Jaso was. "And Erroll says, 'What are you talking about, we won by 60!' And they said to him, 'Effing Jaso, we coulda scored a hundred points tonight, and he took his foot off the gas!' You really can't win."

Both Jaso and Lara showed a dedication to getting kids scholarships, which they feel is a big part of the true legacy of the program. "Are we really doing it for the championships?" asked Lara. "When we win a championship, all I feel is a load coming off my back—it's just not worrying for a minute. And then people immediately start asking if you're doing it again the next year. To me, it's getting these kids to succeed. And we've done that. Poly has always done that. Jurrell Casey does not go to the NFL if [academic coach] Monica Kim doesn't help him study to pass his SAT. But people don't see that."

The years that followed the 2008 title saw time-honored Poly traditions fall. First, the team lost to Lakewood in 2009, breaking its state-record league winning streak. Then, in 2010, it lost a first-round playoff game to Mater Dei, failing to advance to at least the second round for the first time since 1990. At the time of this book's writing, the world of high school football has vastly changed from where it was even five or ten years ago. In the Trinity League (made up of all private Catholic schools, including Mater Dei and Orange Lutheran), more than half of the head football coaches draw six-figure salaries. Most of them do not teach, coaching full-time, year-round. At Poly, future NFL pros are still training on the same dirt oval that Willie McGinest and Gene Washington spilled sweat into. Lara is still making his $5,000 Long Beach Unified School District (LBUSD) coaching stipend and pulling graveyard duty as a probation officer.

It hardly makes sense, frankly, that the school is still so competitive. In 2010–2011, ESPN once again named Poly the top sports school in the country, despite budget shortfalls and other obstacles. It's no wonder the nationally televised documentary series *4th and Forever* was put together to try and figure out what makes the school tick. Just about every major national sports media outlet has been around, at one point or another, to do the same.

It's a question worth examining.

The Legacy

This chapter presents a reasonably comprehensive detailing of Long Beach Poly's football history. Yet that chronicle still feels incomplete, for it's a lengthy accounting of the program's "what," with not much investigation of "why." Why has one inner-city public school been able to maintain such a level of excellence despite being outspent by its competition one hundred to one? Why has the school excelled and overcome the obstacles of a changing world? Why are its players so damn *fast*?

It's a question that deserves some consideration before leaving 1600 Atlantic and moving to other parts of the city. As the *Cal Hi Almanac* says:

> *While most perennial powers go through cycles of producing high-level talent, or produce D1 caliber players for a number of seasons before demographics or coaching changes stop the harvests, one school that has been consistently producing talent since 1985 and well before that is Long Beach Poly.*

Certainly the storyline is powerful and its own motivation. Public v. private, minority v. majority, poor v. rich—the David v. Goliath theme is one that resonates throughout the world of sports and daily American life. That accessibility is at least partially responsible for the school's popularity. When I was traveling in Austin, Texas, a cab driver taking me from the airport was surprised to hear that I was a sportswriter from Long Beach and asked if I covered Poly football. When I told him I did, he told me, "That's my favorite team."

I asked him if he was an alumnus, and he said no, that he had never seen the team play in person and had never, in fact, been to Southern California. But he learned about the school during the rivalry years with Mater Dei, was heartbroken when it lost to De La Salle and checked on how it did every Saturday morning during football season. He felt that the school, halfway across the country, stood for something that he stood for, that it had lived through things he had lived through.

The history is also self-propelling. When I was bringing a large photo back onto campus after having scanned it, a linebacker from the 2011 team saw me (Matt Rowe, the third of three Rowe linebackers to get Divison 1 scholarships out of the school) and asked what I was carrying. I told him it was a group shot of the 1919 team and, without hesitating, Rowe asked, "Wasn't that the first team to go undefeated and win state?"

Kids at Poly all seem to have that understanding of where their school came from, what it's accomplished. As a high school sportswriter, that's a strange and refreshing phenomenon. And to members of the Poly community, knowing that all those eye-popping accomplishments exist (709 wins after the 2011 season, the most in California history, and sixty-four NFL players, most of any school in the nation) means something. I'm not sure what, but it means something.

I asked every person I interviewed what was responsible for Poly's continued success and what it meant. Every one of them had something different to say.

Raul Lara said the legacy of the school was in the kids it helped along. In the modern era alone, from Barnett's first year, the school has gotten well over 150 players Division 1 scholarships, keys to free educations that have changed the course of families. No other team in the state comes close. On the 2001 team alone, a record-breaking 28 players would eventually become Division 1. In 1998, there were 24—those are the two most scholarship-laden teams in state history.

There is also the family element; every year, nearly a half-dozen players on the team had fathers who played for the team back in the day and grandfathers who played for the team *way* back in the day.

Coaching great Dave Levy said that the importance of talent cannot be discounted. "Raw talent is just huge. And the community goes out for the team—it's a combination of those things."

Don Norford, who's been a coach since 1976, said, "The community was determined to keep Poly clean, and to make it special."

Daily-Lyles has another angle. When asked what age he was when he knew he would play for Poly, he answered six. "Seriously," he said, "it was like destiny. Everyone in my family went to this school; I was talking about it by fifth grade. By the time I got here, I knew all the coaches, all the buildings. It's a special place—if you have pride in something, it can carry you through each era, whether there's racial changes, socio-economic changes, or changes on the football field."

"Is it in the water?" Dee Andrews speculated. "I don't know. But these same kids are from fathers like us—the apples don't fall far from the tree." Andrews certainly knows that to be true. His daughter, Brandi, is married to Poly athletic director Rob Shock, and his granddaughters own as much Poly gear as any die-hard fan.

Jeff Turley, a defensive coordinator on the last four championship teams, said, "The diversity this campus provides is one of the reasons why I had my kids come here. It allows changes to go on without losing focus on tradition. Everybody in sports talks about tradition, and people would kill for the kind we have here."

Jerry Jaso sees it as keeping a particular kind of spirit alive, and protected. "There's a culture at Poly that's endemic to the place. That's unique. And if you honor that culture and feed that culture, you'll have more success than if you go in as an outsider and say, 'Okay we're going to change everything.' There's a right way and a wrong way of doing it."

The impact on the NFL and pro level is undeniable. Everyone likes to tout the "most NFL players of any high school" stat around Poly, but the impact that players like Gene Washington, Willie McGinest, DeSean Jackson and the other sixty-one men have had is impossible to sum up. There were three white Poly players on the first Green Bay Packers championship team in 1929, and players like Washington helped redefine the role of black players in the sports world decades later.

Poly players have been named to 15 NFL Pro Bowls and have been a part of 9 NFL championships. Four have been named Rookie of the Year. Jackrabbits in the NFL have recovered 98 fumbles, sacked 113 quarterbacks and even kicked three field goals. They've scored 336 NFL touchdowns, gained over 40,000 yards receiving (and counting, thanks to Marcedes Lewis, DeSean Jackson, Terrence Austin and other Poly pass-catchers who will play in 2012). The 64 Poly players who have gone on to the NFL have played 239 seasons of NFL football among them, and hundreds more have been played in the Canadian Football League and other minor US leagues.

The Jackrabbits won CIF titles in 1919, 1923, 1927, 1929, 1930, 1934, 1936, 1958, 1959, 1980, 1985, 1997, 1999, 2000, 2001, 2004, 2007 and 2008. Ask a hundred former players, coaches, writers and historians what is behind the school's run of dominance across so many different eras and you'll probably get two hundred answers. Poly guys like to talk, after all. But a backup lineman on a team from a few years ago who was asked that question may have had the best answer. He scoffed and said, "It's just Poly, man. It was made to be the best—and it is."

CHAPTER TWO

Don Norford

The Godfather

Although he has never been the head football coach at Long Beach Poly, no accounting of that team's history would be complete without talking about Don Norford, affectionately known around the campus and community as "Papa Don."

Norford grew up one block from Poly and never got much farther away than that. He graduated in 1964 and began coaching Pop Warner football in 1971. Five years later, he made his way back to his alma mater, as a football assistant and a track coach. Since 1976, Norford has been coaching with the football team every fall and running the track team every spring. He has coached every single position on the football team at one point or another.

The results are astounding. He was an assistant on nine of the eighteen CIF champion football teams Poly had. On the track, where he has mentored many football speedsters, the results are even more staggering. Norford has his name listed as the head coach of seventeen California state track championship teams, between the boys' and girls' programs, as well as an outstanding thirty-five CIF Southern Section championships. In all, that is seventy CIF section and state championships in thirty-six years of coaching.

When Jackrabbits are asked what makes Poly special, Norford comes up often. If you listen to the testimonials of some of the players he worked with who went on to pro careers, you can understand why. Mark Carrier, NFL Rookie of the Year in 1990 and currently a Bengals' coach, said, "I owe that man a lot. Don came into my life right when I needed it. He was a father figure and he was a disciplinarian. He taught me how to succeed."

Willie McGinest, the three-time Super Bowl champ with the Patriots, said, "Don Norford really taught me how to play. He taught me how to be relentless on the field and how to never stop working hard. He'll never take the credit, though." In truth, Norford could take a lot of credit for McGinest's career. At his induction to the Poly Football Hall of Fame, the former Patriot recalled that when he had arrived on campus, he intended to just play basketball. It was Norford who took one look at him and said, "You're playing football."

So renowned were his technical instructions that Long Beach couldn't keep him a secret, and word spread about his workouts, from Poly alums in the NFL. Over time, Norford had other NFL pros like Jason Taylor, Brandon Lloyd and TJ Houshmandzadeh working with him in the offseason. His status as a conduit for NFL talent earned him the NFL's High School Football Coach of the Year Award in 1996, the only time in history an assistant has won that honor. It came with a $5,000 prize check, which Norford immediately cashed and deposited into Poly's athletics fund.

More than his technical instruction, though, his value to the school has been as a mentor and a father figure. Before his wife of thirty-seven years, Carol, passed away in 2003, their home on Easy Avenue was constantly filled with Poly players who came for a meal and sometimes stayed longer. Poly greats like Darrell Rideaux and Marquez Pope, among many others, lived with the Norfords at some point in their high school career, either to help focus on school and sports or because of a turbulent situation at home.

Norford said that while his role is well known around Long Beach, his wife doesn't get enough credit. "Don't let 'em fool you, she could cook," he laughed. "She might have been more of an influence than me—because kids would open up to her and then she would let me know what was going on, and I would know how to talk to them."

The coach, who said he's nearing the end of his long, storied run, is an indelible link to the school's past. He recalled leaving Roosevelt Elementary and climbing onto the Poly campus with his friends, hiding behind a mulberry bush to watch Dee Andrews and Willie Brown run in track meets. That was a big part of why he knew at such a young age that he would end up at the school. "You weren't a man if you didn't go to Poly," he said. He said his way of relating to kids is simple and easy to replicate. "I always mixed coaching with life. If I corrected them, I would try to relate it to a life situation so they could understand it, and I made sure kids knew I was always available to talk to me one-on-one, that I would listen. That's it."

Though he could have seven championship rings for every finger, Norford said that the people he's worked with meant more to him than any jewelry. In fact, he said he doesn't even know where most of his rings are. "My nieces and nephews have run off with them," he said. "The relationships I have with the athletes, that's more treasured to me than anything else. That's what I cherish."

There was one moment the humble Papa Don got to share with Carol that got through to him, though. At the NFL banquet for his coach of the year award, Norford recalled, "We were sitting down, and it was gold everything. Gold plate, gold cups, everything. And me and my wife looked at each other and were like, 'Oh wow, we're royalty!'"

To fans of Long Beach football, Don and Carol Norford truly are.

CHAPTER THREE

VETERANS MEMORIAL STADIUM

Home of Long Beach Football

Underneath Veterans Memorial Stadium, there is a Freedom Shrine. It consists of a dozen or so facsimile copies of some of the greatest documents in America's history, from the Gettysburg Address to the Declaration of Independence. They were placed there by the International Exchange Club, with the goal of "Strengthening our appreciation of our American heritage." Ironically, few players today are aware of the incredible heritage and history of the building itself.

To many football players now, Vets is simply there. Indeed, if you were to walk into the stadium for the first time, it would be easy to overlook its unique history because it isn't really showcased. There is a plaque, reading: "Veterans Memorial Stadium: Dedicated in humble gratitude to those who died in war that we may live in peace." Next to that plaque should be another, with a tear sheet from the February 25, 1945 edition of the *Press-Telegram.* On its cover is printed an appeal from seventeen Long Beach soldiers and former high school football players writing from overseas during the final months of World War II. The missive is headlined, "An Open Letter—Think It Over!!" and is addressed from South Pacific, where the Long Beach soldiers were stationed. It reads:

Dear Long Beach:

We were thinking of you last night!

As we lay in our "bunks" last night, we were thinking of the fun of just walking up and down a crowded Pine Ave on a Saturday afternoon and peering in the windows, of getting a sandwich or a malt at one of those drive-ins, of seeing Poly or Wilson or Jordan on the athletic field, or being down on the beach swimming, eating hot dogs, relaxing.

You see—we were thinking of you last night. We were thinking of home!!!

And then our thoughts became reminiscent—of friends, of other days. We all want to be HOME again, that's the day we're living for.

But our thoughts weren't just those, when would we be going home, for we remembered Billy. Everyone at Wilson knew Billy. What a swell kid. Well, he wouldn't be going home. Neither will Jay. Poly students can still remember his speeches in assembly. And then there's Walt and Dick and Bob and Eddie and Truman, and we could go on and on. Everyone in Long Beach knows them. They won't be going home, not tomorrow, next month, or forever. And forever is an awfully long time. They've gone over the final yard marker—to the horizons beyond, and they went there for YOU and for ME.

They weren't in this thing because of the glamour attached to a gunner's wings; the pay the captain drew didn't make being away from home half worthwhile enough; or the tow-headed kid you knew down the street, he wasn't getting seasick night after night on the high seas because he thought he was another Columbus.

No, the fact remains, they, your boys, all Sons of Long Beach, were out here because they believed in fighting for the American way of living, and the right to go back and to enjoy the kind of home they'd known in Long Beach.

This war won't last forever!

And when it's over, memories will become shortened of what Billy, Jay, Walt, Dick, Bob, Eddie and Truman gave for you and for me. They gave all they had—their life. To us that's a pretty big order; our boys, Sons of Long Beach, have given and are giving their lives, that we may win this war.

Had they lived, had they gone home, we think they would have wanted more than a giant, modern tank, circled with a chain fence in Lincoln Park, and a plaque commemorating Long Beach's Second World War Dead.

They would have wanted a "living" commemoration of what their deeds and sacrifices and valor gave to Long Beach; they would have wanted something that every time one of Long Beach's citizenry viewed or used it, they would know over and over again, that these were the things they gave their lives for—the right to laugh and be gay, to gather and play, to grow healthy and strong and to meet on the field of sports, rather than ever again, the field of war.

They died for YOU AND ME!

We propose that we build a sports stadium in Long Beach, after the war when materials are available. We've needed one for a long time. We propose that this stadium, built with your and our funds, dedicated to those who "went beyond the final yard marker," would be a living memorial for them, where the young and old alike could gather for sports, for civic affairs and for fun and joy. This would be their wish.

Long Beach, we know you shall not fail those who have given their lives for us. Enclosed is our $75 contribution to Long Beach's Memorial Stadium...dedicated to those who gave their lives that others might live.

Send in your contribution to a real worth-while cause. Don't put it off. Do it today! Large or small, the amount will help to build a Long Beach Memorial Stadium that will live as a tribute to those who have made the greatest sacrifice of all.

We'll be seeing you in Long Beach's Memorial Stadium after the war.

The letter was signed by: Jim Lineberger (Poly '37), Jim Michaels (Poly '37), Al Brainard (Poly '36), El Leonard (Poly '37), A.J. O'Hara (Poly '37), Joe Skeber (Poly '36), Vancil Martin (Poly '37), Irvin Meairs (Wilson '41), Ray Davis (Wilson '36), Stan Durfer (Poly '38), Jack Carlson (Poly '39), Lewis Lacy (Poly '38), Harold Hofman (Poly '36), Bill Case (Poly '39), Bob Lorden (Poly '40), Stan Davidson (Poly '40) and Tommy Milovitch (Poly '37).

Long Beach, a city that has always been willing to put its money where its mouth is when it comes to civic improvements, passed a $550,000 bond the next year, authorizing the funds to build the stadium, which was to be located on the Long Beach City College campus. After that passionately written request and, after the soldiers (still at war) chipped in some of their military stipends, how could Long Beach have denied them?

By 1948 the city had come up with a design and broken ground and, two years later, construction was complete, and the stadium was ready to host its first high school football game in 1950. Lineberger, one of the signees who had played football at Poly and who would go on to a long, successful refereeing career, was coaching at Wilson that year. He led his Bruins to a 13–12 victory over his alma mater.

In the intervening seventy-two years, the venerable old stadium has been used for hundreds of high school football games, most notably serving as the home field of the Poly Jackrabbits, as well as the LBCC Vikings. It's also played host to many nonfootball events, including track meets, motorcycle rallies and graduations.

Vets under construction, 1948. *LBCC yearbook.*

Long Beach's football palace today. *Photo by the author.*

Vets has also been a public face of Long Beach as the star of innumerable commercials, TV shows and movies (just last year, Vets appeared in ads for Nike and Gatorade). But perhaps the only event guaranteed to match the explosiveness and flash of a high school football game is the annual Fourth of July fireworks show, attended by thousands of Long Beach citizens.

The stadium, which is now owned by Long Beach City College, was built by the people and for the people and is an intricate part of the city. Every citizen who lived in Long Beach in the era it was built had a hand (or a dollar) in its construction. In fact, even that simple dedication on the plaque was written by a Long Beach resident, Nellie B. McClellan. She was the chosen winner out of 188 entries in a dedication-writing contest.

CHAPTER FOUR

Long Beach Wilson

The Bad News Bruins

The CIF's official football record book contains twenty-four pages, and, despite the fact that Long Beach Wilson (the city's second high school) was founded in 1926, the Bruins have their names recorded just one time in those record books. And it wasn't good news, either—it's because Poly quarterback Chris Lewis threw seven touchdowns against the Bruins in his sophomore season, the third-best single-game total in CIF history.

In fact, among football historians, Wilson has a reputation for being one of the oldest schools in Southern California to have never competed for a CIF football championship. "Didn't even come close, I believe," remarked CIF historian John Dahlem. Any book about the history of aquatic sports in Long Beach or baseball would feature a Wilson section at the front as long as the Poly chapter in this book. But football simply hasn't been the Bruins' sport. That doesn't mean that they haven't produced some phenomenal athletes. In fact, they are one of the city's best remembered football teams.

The Bruins first fielded a football team in 1926, and Oak Smith was their coach. Smith, who could be nicknamed as the Originator, would leave the school after the 1927 season to open another football tradition at Long Beach City College (LBCC). Cliff Meyer was the first quarterback for Wilson, who were known as the Bears when the school first opened. Smitty Smitheran scored the first touchdown in school history, and both the Meyer and Smitheran families would send several generations of student-athletes to Wilson over the decades.

The best individual player of the early days was probably "Cowboy" Joe Forbes, the punter, who was famous for being able to punt over the entire Wilson campus. He averaged fifty yards per punt at Wilson and then went to LBCC, where he averaged sixty. He then moved on to Occidental and actually averaged over seventy yards per punt for a season, earning All-American honors.

According to Wilson legend Skip Rowland, who spoke to the *Press-Telegram*'s Bob Keisser a few years before his passing, it took six years for Wilson to begin playing its crosstown rivals, Long Beach Poly, because, "They were fearful the game would cause too many problems. They were right."

The rivalry was quickly dubbed "The Big Game," and while other rivalries in Long Beach have come and gone, this one has stayed fresh, even in recent years as the games haven't been as competitive. In 1932, they played their first game, ending in a 0–0 tie that sparked a riot on the field, which was only halted by the school turning the sprinklers on and playing "The Star Spangled Banner."

Poly defeated the Bruins year after year at the start of the teams' series, with Wilson not scoring a touchdown until 1936, when All-CIF fullback Norm Standlee plunged across the goal line. Standlee went on to a career at Stanford and then had an eight-year NFL career with the Bears and 49ers. Coach Al Johnson had taken the coaching reigns in 1936, a move that would help shape the next decade of Wilson history. By 1938, The Big Game was so big that Long Beach's city limits couldn't even hold it, and the game was moved to the Rose Bowl, where 30,000 fans watched Poly defeat Wilson yet again, this time 19–0.

Finally, in 1943, on their twelfth try, things would change for the Bruins. The game was played at Poly's Burcham Field, with Meyer, the team's first captain and quarterback, serving as an assistant coach to Johnson. The quarterback of the 1943 Jinx Busters was Jimmy Eccles, and stars included Dick Ottele, Johnny Mann, Keith Deeds, Dick Bowdey and Skip Rowland. Ten thousand fans gathered at the stadium while World War II occupied most people's thoughts and concerns.

In a commemorative article written by the *Press-Telegram*'s Doug Krikorian several decades later, Lyle Brown, a fullback, remembered,

> *There were so many Wilson grads on the sidelines in uniform, including my brother Ed who played in the 1938 game. It was weird in those days. It seemed like every young man who wasn't going to high school was in a military uniform. When you got out of high school, it was almost automatic you went into the service.*

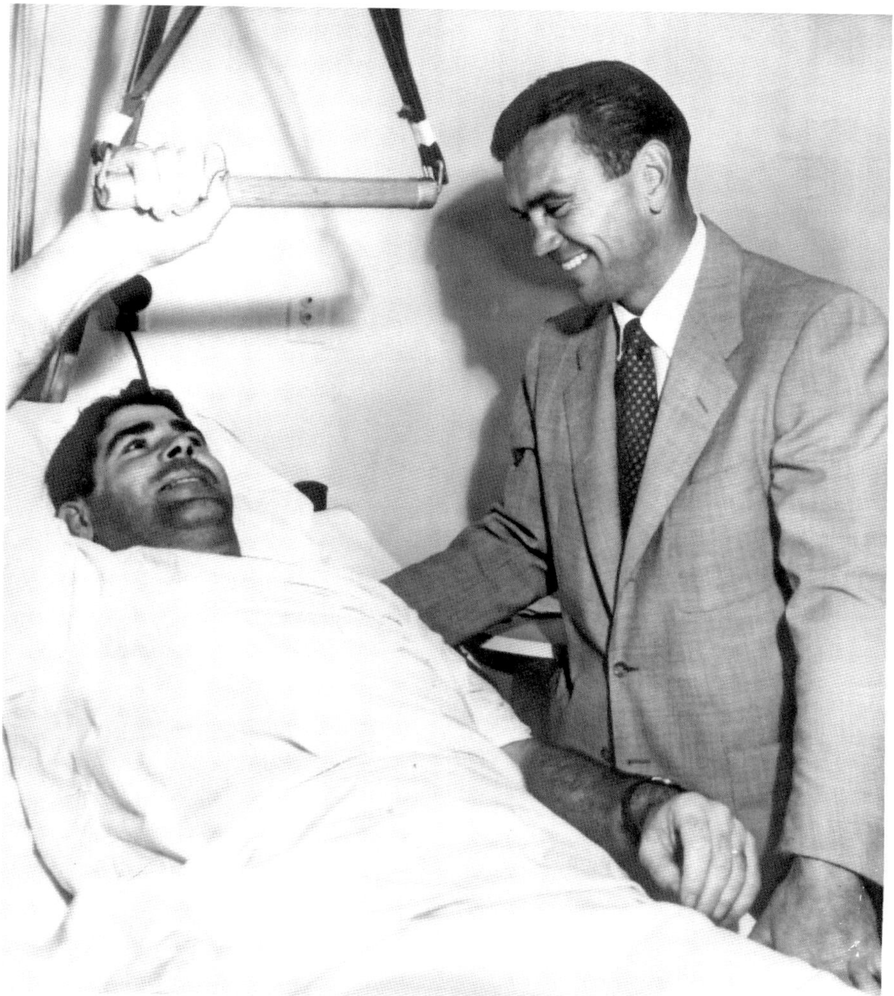

Wilson standout Norm Standlee in the hospital. Standlee was a mid-1930s star for the Bruins, but injuries hampered his collegiate career. *Courtesy* Press-Telegram.

The Bruins went up 14–7 at halftime, and Johnson asked his team for another two scores to bring the game home. It delivered that and more, as Rowland and leading rusher John Mann (101 yards) proved too much for the Jackrabbits. The final score was Wilson 37, Poly 7, and the clock ticking down to 00:00 set off a celebration befitting of a national championship.

"The one thing about that Jinx Busters team," said longtime *Press-Telegram* columnist and local sports historian Bob Keisser, "they were clearly the better team. The myth of the Jinx Busters is true to an extent, except that they *should* have won that game."

The team paraded down Pine Avenue and marched into theaters across the city, celebrating on stage with its fans. As the Bruins marched, fans and coaches and cheerleaders marched with them, waving pompoms and singing, "Wilson, Woodrow Wilson, finest school in the land." That night, as the celebration extended to an all-night dance on the streets of Belmont Shore, there was no doubt that it was. After, soldiers from all over Europe and the Pacific who had played at Wilson telegrammed their congratulations.

It was a victory that would live forever in Wilson's collective consciousness. Johnson told Krikorian many years later, "The times...oh, they have changed. But the memories don't. The years don't take them away, thank God."

Johnson would coach for a decade, winning seven baseball titles in addition to his football success. He's a member of the Century Club and Long Beach Baseball Halls of Fame. Rowland was the most successful player from that team, going on to star in football and baseball at UCLA, before returning to Wilson to coach the baseball, football and golf teams for several decades and winning twenty-four Moore League titles. Rowland is a member of the Wilson Hall of Fame, the Long Beach Century Club Hall of Fame, the UCLA Hall of Fame, the UCLA Baseball Hall of Fame, the Long Beach Baseball Hall of Fame and the CIF Hall of Fame.

There is no doubt that the 1943 team occupies an enormous place in Wilson's history. But many individual players and coaches created memories as well. There was coach Jim Lineberger, who was a Poly grad who crossed sidelines to hold the clipboard at Wilson. After leaving the Bruins, Lineberger went on to a successful career as a Pac-10 referee and a full-time officiating career. He was even one of the officials at the 1970 Pasadena Bowl, the only bowl game Long Beach State ever competed in. Lineberger was the coach of the Bruins between Johnson and Rowland and led the Bruins to a 13–12 victory over Poly in the first game played at Vets Stadium.

Great players of the era included Carl Fennema (later National Player of the Year with Compton College) and Doug Brown (who played for Fresno State and later the Raiders and Rams). The year 1957 was the first year of the Moore League, and Wilson won the title after beating Poly 26–14 in front of ten thousand, followed by its defeat of Jordan, 12–7. But the Bruins lost all of their preseason games and bowed out in the first round of CIF, finishing with an overall record of 4–5.

Despite featuring one of the school's most talented rosters, 1960 ended in disappointment after the undefeated Bruins suffered a shocking loss to

Al Johnson, providing instruction to an early Wilson team. *Courtesy* Press-Telegram.

Skip Rowland at UCLA, five years after the "Jinx Busters" game. *Courtesy* Press-Telegram.

Coach Jim Lineberger, who would later serve as an NCAA official, with wife Dottie. *Courtesy* Press-Telegram.

Riverside Poly in the first round of CIF, 47–12. The loss was "one of the most humiliating in the school's history. Old Bruins couldn't remember when Wilson looked so sluggish," one newspaper said. That year, Bob Bailey was the team's All-CIF quarterback. It was also Carl Peterson's senior year. Peterson had one of the city's longest and most successful careers in football. After Wilson, Peterson went on to UCLA but really made his mark starting in 1988, when he was hired by Lamar Hunt as the president and general manager of the Kansas City Chiefs, a role he remained in until 2008. Since, Peterson has been the chairman of USA Football, helping to provide leadership to youth football initiatives across the country. His work in football earned him the 2012 Pete Rozelle Award, previously awarded to Bill Walsh, Vince Lombardi and Pat Summerall, among others.

The next year, Wilson won the Moore League title again, making 1960 and 1961 the only back-to-back Moore League titles in school history. Rowland once again piloted his team to an undefeated regular season, defeating Poly

Carl Peterson, a Wilson player who went on to a two-decade long NFL front office career, including a long stint as the general manger of the Chiefs. *Courtesy* Press-Telegram.

Dennis Dummit, a star quarterback at Wilson, LBCC and UCLA, taking a run on the beach. *Courtesy* Press-Telegram.

Jeff Severson, an All-Star player who went on to star at Long Beach State and with the LA Rams. *Wilson yearbook.*

21–20 before a crowd of 17,000. Ed Doll returned the opening kickoff 85 yards for a touchdown and later kicked the game-winning PAT. But once again, the Bruins were bounced in the first round of the playoffs, extending their playoff win drought to 16 years.

In Rowland's final season, in 1963, he took the Bruins to their best-ever playoff finish, with the team making it all the way to the semifinals. Other star players in the 1960s included Sid Smith, who was an All-CIF tackle who went on to a four-year NFL career with the Chiefs and Oilers; and Dennis Dummit, the school's best ever quarterback. Dummit was an All-American at LBCC and then set fourteen passing records at UCLA, some of which are still standing.

In 1976, Wilson beat Poly 21–16 while being coached by Jon Meyer, the son of Bruins' first captain, Cliff. (Jon's son Scott would become defensive coordinator three decades later). The school's Moore League success has been lacking in the sport; it won only seven titles and just one since 1978, when the Bruins steamrolled their competition in 1991. One of the most lastingly visible members of the Wilson alumni community has been safety Jeff Severson, who played for the school in the mid- to late 1960s, before going on to Long Beach State, where he played for the only team to make a bowl game appearance. He played in a Super Bowl his rookie season with the Redskins, who were coached by Hall of Fame coach George Allen, and he had a six-year NFL career. His retirement in Long Beach has seen him gain acclaim as an actor, comedian and performer, the "Singing Safety."

It's worth noting that, were they in a different league, the Bruins would quite possibly have won a championship. For many decades, though, only league champions advanced to the postseason, which limited Wilson's opportunities, thanks in part to having to share the Moore League with Poly. Poly's Mike Giers recalled a few years during the 1950s when Poly was ranked one and Wilson two but, even though the Bruins beat a few other highly ranked teams, they didn't make the playoffs because they weren't league champs. "By today's rules," Giers said, "when multiple teams get to go, I'm pretty sure we would have played them for a championship."

The rivalry itself may have hurt Wilson's chances, too, according to Severson.

"The coaches' goal was always to beat Poly, not win CIF," he said. "And over the years, people have been maybe too focused on that. It should have been 'let's win CIF, and we'll beat Poly on the way.'"

Much of the luster of Wilson's tradition in football lies in its longevity and the great memories of teams and players that have been created. It hasn't hoisted a CIF championship trophy, but no history of Long Beach would be complete without a trip down Bruin memory lane. Or, as Skip Rowland put it more eloquently in a 1990 article about the history of Wilson and Poly's rivalry, providing advice to modern players taking part in the tradition:

> *Shake down the thunder from the Long Beach skies and you'll find stars galore. Wake up the echoes and you'll hear the cheers of thousands of appreciative football fans. Thanks to the players in the past and good luck to the players of today and future years. It's 48 minutes to play, a lifetime to remember.*

CHAPTER FIVE

HARRY J. MOORE

The Boss of Bosses

In the entire CIF Southern Section, there is only one athletic league that's named after a person. Leagues are usually named after geographical features or regional locations. There is even the industrially named Freeway League. But there's only one league named after a person, because there was only one Harry J. Moore.

Moore has since passed away, but his legacy in Long Beach and around the CIF is cemented, thanks to the Harry J. Moore League, the league that contains all of the Long Beach public high schools. The league was created in 1957, after Millikan and Lakewood opened, giving the area enough teams to form a league. Teams have come and gone over the years, but Poly, Wilson, Jordan, Lakewood, Millikan and Compton have been steady members. In recent years, Cabrillo was added to the league. In football, after the 2011 season, Poly had won thirty-eight titles; Lakewood had won nine; Wilson had won seven; Millikan, four; Compton, four; ex-member El Rancho, four; and Jordan, three, all of which were tied.

Players today may not have a good sense of who Moore was, however. In doing historical research, his name pops up over and over. In fact, it's difficult to imagine what the modern world of high school sports would look like without Moore's influence. He was a Poly administrator from 1919–30 and principal of Wilson from 1932–47, before becoming assistant superintendent of LBUSD from 1947–57. He retired shortly before the league in his name was created.

He was also a founding member of the CIF and its president for thirty-four years, from 1920–54, and he instituted such revolutionary ideas as

Harry J Moore. Moore was an administrator at Poly, a principal at Wilson, a CIF president for over thirty years and the man for whom Long Beach's sports league is named. *Courtesy* Press-Telegram.

moving the age limit for prep athletes down to nineteen (it had been twenty-one previously). He actually attempted to resign from the organization after Poly was temporarily expelled in 1920, saying that if the CIF wouldn't have Poly as a member, he would assume it didn't want him either. The CIF's board refused to accept his resignation, so he served even during the year when the school he worked for wasn't a member.

Long Beach's high school sports league isn't the only important piece of Southern California sports that bears Moore's name, however. He and Poly donated the Harry J. Moore Trophy to the CIF, the organization's first perpetual championship trophy for football. The trophy is no longer used and sits on display in the historical archives section of the CIF office. Thanks to the league that bears his name, Moore's memory remains in circulation, however.

CHAPTER SIX

LONG BEACH CITY COLLEGE

The Conquering Vikings

The role of junior college sports in the modern world is difficult to determine. Very few schools can draw the kinds of crowds that they would have fifty years ago and, more and more, junior college programs are seen as a pit stop between high school and four-year programs, more often a place for athletes to get their grades up than an end in and of itself. But there was a time when that wasn't the case, when Long Beach City College was the city's favorite college football team, made up entirely of local players. "We didn't know anything about Cerritos or Fullerton," said Dee Andrews, one of many Long Beach high school stars to move on to LBCC. "This was Long Beach, and we all went there, from all the high schools."

The Vikings were generally awful, but when they were good, they were unbelievable. In fact, they were the winners of five national championships and the bearers of Long Beach's proud banner.

EARLY YEARS

The original plan was for Long Beach City College to open in 1916, but the First World War put a pin in that. Eventually, the school would open its doors in 1927. Or rather, it would open the doors of Wilson High, and its

The first football team at LBCC, 1928. *LBCC yearbook.*

recently constructed campus served as LBCC's home base for the first eight years, until the college could build its own location. In 1927, the school had two coaches: Bert Smith, who ran the basketball team, and Oak Smith, who coached football (making him the first head coach of both Wilson High and LBCC). Bert Smith captured state titles in basketball in 1928 and 1929, giving them a nice head start on the football team, which struggled early. Oak Smith coached the team for its first seven years, and while success did not come for a few decades (it didn't win its first conference title until 1946), the creation of the Vikings' football team brought with it all of the usual excitement and pomp and circumstance.

An excerpt from a yearbook of the time reads:

> *That unconquerable spirit which characterized the history of the Norsemen of olden times entered the sport history of the Vikings of the present age as the predominant quality of the Long Beach Junior College football warriors of 1928. An inferior team in ability and experience, they inaugurated their first season with a never-say-die attitude.*

Not bad for a team that was a hair's breadth from going winless, before scoring late in games against Glendale and Pasadena to turn the tables.

The Vikings' first two coaches, Oak Smith (right) and Mel Griffin (left). *Courtesy* Press-Telegram.

Quarterback Dalton Mobley was the team's captain for the first two years, leading it to a winning season in 1929 when the team went 5–4. The Vikings were also victorious over UCLA's freshman team and had a 9–7 victory over defending conference champion Pasadena.

Already a rivalry after just two seasons (mostly because of the existing hatred between the two schools), former Wilson star Cliff Meyer keyed the upset in the Poly v. Pasadena game with an eight-yard touchdown and the game's winning field goal as well, kicked with just two minutes left in the game.

The team was known in its early decades for its fighting spirit, and that fighting spirit led lineman "Babe" Fraser to break his leg in a 1932 game against Compton. Fraser had to spend "many months" in the hospital. That same year, the team would play Taft in its first-ever night game, winning 6-0.

After Smith, Mel Griffin and Harry Macon had their turns coaching the Vikings, the school made a coaching decision in 1938 that reads more like a hire from recent years than a late 1930s strategy. They hired Orian Landreth, the legendary coach of four CIF titles at Long Beach Poly (recently returned from a sour one-year stint coaching Arizona) with the hope that former Jackrabbits would be lured to the school. Landreth stayed only the one year as football coach, serving instead as LBCC's dean of sports. But the move worked. The 1939 team he coached finished 5–3–2 overall and marked the Vikings best-ever finish in conference play, at second place, a mark they equaled in 1940.

The momentum continued to build through 1942, when the team was 5–2–1 and, once again, second only to one in the conference standings. But then football, like most of life in Long Beach, was put on hold because of World War II. Just as World War I had delayed the school's opening, World War II delayed the football ascendance of the Vikings, and they suspended their program because there simply weren't enough students on campus to form a football team. After the war ended, they picked up right where they left off, winning six games in 1945, the most in school history to that point.

The 1946 team, coached by Eddie Wagner, would bring home the first championship in the school's eighteen-year history in the sport. The Vikings were made up of war-returnees, Long Beach players who had come home happy to turn their postwar energies onto the gridiron. Joe Ricobono was one of the best, helping to lead the team to a 9–2 record and a conference title. The team just missed an invitation to the Junior Rose Bowl (which pitted the nation's two best junior college teams against each other every year for a national title) thanks to a 20–18 loss to Compton, which scored 20 points toward the end of the game. The team is still ranked one of LBCC's best, however, ten players having gone on to Division 1 institutions.

True glory was just a few years away. Wagner left the team to teach at the newly opened Pacific Coast campus of LBCC after the 1948 season, closing a successful tenure but also paving the way for Grant "Buck" Andreasen to take over. With Long Beach's first real football palace,

The first Long Beach Poly football team was also Long Beach's first high school team and the first team of any kind to play a full, organized schedule. *Poly yearbook.*

Poly's 1919 championship team, considered the best team in Long Beach's history. These players won CIF, state and southwestern championships. *Poly archives.*

Morley Drury playing for USC in 1927. Called "the Noblest Trojan of Them All," Drury starred at Poly and is still one of the finest players the Jackrabbits ever produced. *Courtesy* Press-Telegram.

Orian Landreth and Al Johnson. Rival coaches (Landreth of Poly and Johnson of Wilson), they are shown here later in life, when they were close friends. Landreth won four CIF titles with Poly while Johnson was head coach of the 1943 Wilson "Jinx Busters" team, the first ever to beat Poly. *Courtesy* Press-Telegram.

Above: Walter "Ray" McCowen in action in 1934. McCowen was the first black football player at Poly and was popular on and off the field. *Poly yearbook*.

Left: Jacques Grenier, the brainy St. Anthony coach who led his team to the 1948 CIF title. *Courtesy* Press-Telegram.

Johnny Olszewski starred at St. Anthony in 1948 and went on to star at Cal and in the NFL. *St. Anthony yearbook.*

Sam Cathcart and his brother, Royal, starred at Poly in the early 1940s. Sam is pictured here in a San Francisco 49ers publicity shot taken in 1949, the year he was named Rookie of the Year. *Courtesy* Press-Telegram.

The Naval Base on Terminal Island had a football team in the early '50s. Here, military officials draw up plans not for invasion but for a scoring play. *Courtesy* Press-Telegram.

Skip Rowland was a star player on Wilson's 1943 "Jinx Busters" team that was the first to beat Poly. He later starred at UCLA in both baseball and football and returned to coach both sports at Wilson. *Courtesy* Press-Telegram.

Opposite, top: The LBCC Vikings, pictured here in their locker room, celebrate their 1950 national championship, the school's first. *LBCC yearbook.*

Opposite, bottom: Lonzo Irvin in 1960. Irvin was one of several Poly players who would lead LBCC to the 1960 national championship, its first in a decade. Irvin is pictured here on his way to the end zone in the 1960 Junior Rose Bowl. *LBCC yearbook.*

Top: Gary Garrison, pictured here with the Chargers, starred at Millikan and LBCC before becoming San Diego State's best-ever receiver. He then went on to spend eleven years with the Chargers. *Courtesy* Press-Telegram.

Left: Bob Davenport was a Jordan fullback who would go on to be a two-time All-American at UCLA. *Courtesy* Press-Telegram.

Coach Ernie Radford took Jordan to its best-ever finish in 1947. *Courtesy* Press-Telegram.

Ben Agajanian, the man who practically invented modern placekicking, shown here at one of his free kicking camps held in Long Beach, which instructed over 10,000 students over the years. *Courtesy* Press-Telegram.

Above: Poly coach Dave Levy in the locker room with one of his star running backs, Dee Andrews. Poly won a CIF title that year (1958), and Andrews went on to star at LBCC and Long Beach State. *Courtesy* Press-Telegram.

Left: Willie Brown, shown here with the Los Angeles Rams, was another star running back on the Poly title teams of the late '50s. *Courtesy* Press-Telegram.

Cliff Meyer, the first captain and quarterback at Wilson in 1926, went on to a successful coaching career as well. He was a coach on the 1943 "Jinx Busters." *Courtesy* Press-Telegram.

Gene Washington, shown here at Stanford, was a star quarterback and student body president at Poly in the mid-1960s. He went on to a successful college and pro career and rose in the NFL ranks to become director of football operations. *Courtesy* Press-Telegram.

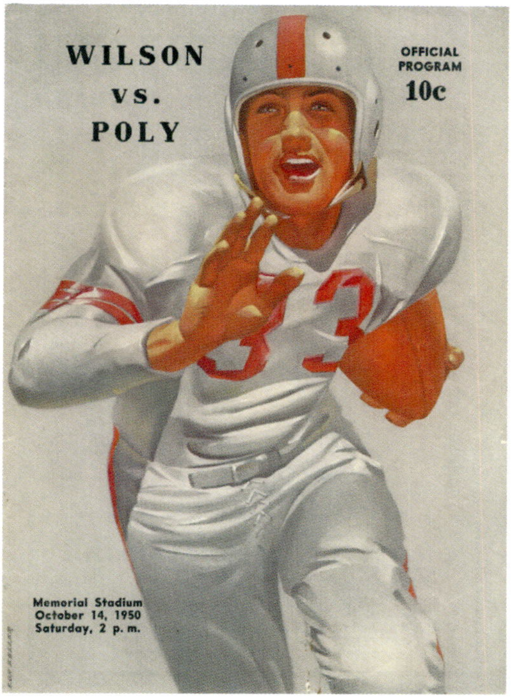

Left: Program from the Wilson/Poly game in 1950, the first high school football game played at Veterans Memorial Stadium. Wilson won 13–12, with Jim Lineberger, a Poly grad who helped get the stadium built, coaching on the sidelines. *Courtesy CIF Southern Section.*

Below: Coach Jim Stangeland is hoisted by his players after winning the 1964 national championship at LBCC. Stangeland coached three national championships there (1960, 1962 and 1964) and would later coach Long Beach State to its only bowl game appearance. *LBCC yearbook.*

Left: Jack Snow with the LA Rams. Snow was an All-CIF receiver at St. Anthony and went on to an All-American career at Notre Dame before playing with the LA Rams for a decade. He is the father of baseball player J.T. Snow. *Courtesy* Press-Telegram.

Below: Long Beach State's team photo from the Pasadena Bowl, the 49ers' only bowl game in school history. They tied with Louisville, 24–24. *Courtesy Long Beach State.*

Left: Long Beach State All-American running back Leon Burns, pictured here in 1970. Burns was a star for the 49ers, but injuries cut his pro career short, and he was killed in an unsolved murder in 1985. *Courtesy Long Beach State.*

Below: Millikan celebrates its 1979 CIF championship after beating Compton 22–21 for the title. *Courtesy CIF Southern Section.*

Left: George Allen on the cover of the 1990 Long Beach State media guide. The Hall of Fame coach's arrival on campus was like Elvis showing up to play a rec center. *Courtesy Long Beach State.*

Below: Promotional materials from Fox Sports Prime Ticket. This is the infamous celebratory ice water bath long said to have killed George Allen. *Courtesy Long Beach State.*

Above: Coach Jerry Jaso played high school football at Poly and would return as a head coach to lead the Jackrabbits to four CIF titles. In his final four years, Poly went 54–1–1 and won three CIF championships. *Poly yearbook.*

Left: Chris Lewis, the finest high school quarterback in Long Beach history. Lewis broke California records for yards and touchdown passes in his senior season. *Poly yearbook.*

Above: Head coach Raul Lara (left), along with his defensive coordinator, Jeff Turley (right), is one of three head coaches to win four CIF titles at Poly. *Courtesy Long Beach Poly.*

Left: DeSean Jackson, a speedy wide receiver at Poly who could have gone pro in baseball, opted for a football career that has already seen him named to two NFL Pro Bowls in his first four seasons. *Courtesy Student Sports.*

Veterans Memorial Stadium, under construction, Andreasen began to construct a team for the ages. In 1949, the team appeared to take a step back, going 4–5–1. But two of its losses were by one point and another by two points.

1950 National Champions

The Vikings lost their first game of the 1950 season—but it should hardly go down as a low moment. After all, the team they were playing was made up of former Viking greats, as the LBCC alumni team defeated the school's 1950 squad 18–6 in the first Vikings game to be played at the newly finished Vets Stadium. But after losing to its forerunners, that year's team would go on to achieve heights that no LBCC team had ever reached.

Led by outstanding players such as Dewey "Hurricane" Tompkins, Jack Prise, Bill Raine, George van Zant, Dick Zimmerman and Dave Levy, the Vikings rolled. Averaging 350 rushing yards per game, they opened with a 20–7 victory over Santa Ana, the first time the Vikings had ever beaten the Dons. Tompkins began his excellent season with an early 52-yard touchdown dash.

They then played Fullerton, a team that had been labeled the "Team of Destiny," and proceeded to beat them 33–2. In a thick fog, they took on Ventura, and they found themselves tied 20–20 with the game winding down and Ventura driving. But, perhaps proving themselves to be the "Team of Destiny" after all, the Vikings rallied. Spence Hanief intercepted a pass and returned it to the 45-yard line. On the next play, with ten seconds remaining, Viking quarterback Jack Price hit receiver Bill Raine for a 55-yard score.

They found themselves tied with San Diego 13–13 the next week, before an offensive explosion gave them a 47–20 victory. They handled the College of the Sequoias the next week, 40–7, as Tompkins broke his own recently set school record by scoring three touchdowns. At that game, the swelling group of Vikings fans began chanting, "Let's go to the Rose Bowl!" and never stopped, as the team continued its incredible march towards the Junior College National championship. The Vikings beat an East Los Angeles team 19–0. They blanked El Camino 32–0, beat rivals Pasadena 13–7 and closed the regular season with a 54–0 win over Santa Monica, holding them to negative sixty-three yards rushing, while the starters hit the benches to rest

The alumni game program in 1950. The Vikings lost to their alums but didn't lose another game all year, claiming the national championship. *LBCC archives.*

Running back Dewey "Hurricane" Tompkins gets his nose busted but keeps plunging forward. *LBCC yearbook.*

before the end of the first quarter. After that, there was no doubt the Vikings belonged in the Junior Rose Bowl.

The city rallied around its Vikings, holding well-attended rallies at Pine and Broadway and around the city to root them on. On December 9, they took the field at the Rose Bowl to play for a national title, in a game broadcast nationally on CBS. Their opponent may have been somewhat intimidating if any of the Vikings had been able to see into the future: they played the Boise College Broncos. The school would go on to become Boise State, a team of national prominence that any junior college team would obviously be proud to have a win over in their record books.

And when the Vikings played Boise in 1950, it was a convincing win, despite the Broncos being undefeated since 1946. The Vikings got an early touchdown from Bill Millington to go up 6–0, and the team led 13–6 after three quarters after a touchdown from Tompkins. The Vikings broke it open in the fourth quarter, scoring on the first play on a fifty-nine-yard touchdown by Bob Brogelman, followed by a thirty-two-yard score from Keith Son. The Broncos scored a last-second Hail Mary to make the score a little more respectable, but the Vikings still came out victorious, 33–13.

Rally before the 1950 Junior Rose Bowl, at Broadway and Pine. *LBCC yearbook.*

Long Beach City College had won the city its first national championship in the sport of football. The city went nuts, and the LBCC campus was so enthralled that a full third of the school yearbook for that year was dedicated to celebrations of its champions. The next year, the Vikings went 8–2–1, with losses to their alumni team again, and to Pasadena, which would get the Junior Rose Bowl nod that season. The year 1952 looked like it might be another championship year, but the Korean War drained the roster, and Andreasen would step down a few years later. In 1956, Cecil Coleman coached the team to a 6–3 record but then left Long Beach to become the

Coach Buck Andreasen is carried off the field after the Vikings won the 1950 Junior Rose Bowl. *LBCC yearbook.*

coach at Arizona State. The next year, the school made two key hires—Long Beach legend Del Walker was brought in as athletic director, and he hired Jim Stangeland to be his football coach.

Stangeland was a supreme motivator, known for hard-driving discipline and innovative motivational techniques. On more than one occasion, he left a fake scouting report in the locker room, with paragraphs badmouthing his own squad, allegedly written by the opposition. He had a modicum of success his first few years, posting two winning records before taking a step back in 1959, going 4–5. But in 1958 and '59, the city's attention was fixed on Long Beach Poly, where former Jackrabbit and Viking Dave Levy was leading a young green and gold team to a pair of back-to-back CIF titles. That group would arrive at LBCC more or less intact the following year. "It was a fabulous era for us," Stangeland recalled. "Fabulous." There's no arguing it—the Vikings would win three national championships in the next five years.

1960 NATIONAL CHAMPIONS

Nobody saw the Vikings coming—except for Long Beach football fans who knew how good players from Poly like tackle Mike Giers, Lonzo Irvin, Willie Martin and Dee Andrews were. The Vikings weren't favored in many of their games early, nor were they winning games by the most convincing margins, either.

They were underdogs to Cerritos in the season opener and trailed 10–8, but they came back to win 25–10. They were expected to lose to Santa Ana and trailed 19–18 late in the game, before quarterback Dave Groff threw an eighty-four-yard pass to Martin, setting up a one-yard touchdown for Irvin. They edged out a 13-8 win over San Diego and a 12–8 victory over El Camino, before finally blowing the doors off a few games, beating Harbor 27–0 and then rolling a loud-talking Bakersfield team, 27–7.

In a torrential downpour at Vets, the Vikings hosted Santa Monica, their fourth undefeated opponent of the season. The Vikings won 51–24 and were rapidly finding their offensive footing in a season that would see them set fifteen offensive records for the school, with a flashy run game that opponents couldn't stop. All five starting linemen were named All-Americans on one list or another, with three running backs receiving honorable mention.

After that, the Vikings beat Valley College 46–20 and were just one win away from a return trip to the Junior Rose Bowl and the bright lights of competing for a national championship. But they trailed East Los Angeles, throwing their hopes into peril. Another comeback gave them a 20–15 victory and another shot at the national title. "Groff came into the huddle before that last drive, and he looks at us, and we've got just a few minutes left," recalled Giers. "And he says, 'Well, we ought to go down and score.' And we went, 'Shit, sounds good!' That's the way that team was."

They were to meet Tyler Junior College in Pasadena that year and try to complete their first-ever undefeated season, since the alumni weren't there to push the Vikings around that year. Stangeland and assistant Paul Chafe flew to Texas to scout Tyler, which still had one game left on its schedule. They arrived in town during a turkey shoot, when the whole town would hunt as one. "We drove into Tyler, and there was this big crowd of people cutting off the road—and they were all carrying rifles," recalled Stangeland. "I turned to Paul and said, 'Goddamn, this is going to be a tough game.'"

It is hard to imagine two more different teams, or cities, than Long Beach and Tyler. The Tyler squad was all white, while the Long Beach

Dee Andrews, one of several offensive stars in 1960, on LBCC's second national championship squad. *LBCC yearbook.*

team was decidedly not, its players having formed a bond at Poly and the other area high schools that transcended race. The difference between the teams was immediately obvious when the Texas players began hurling racial epithets. "There was a linebacker," Dee Andrews recalled. "Every time he'd tackle me, he'd call me a nigger. Every time. And then at halftime, we're coming out of the locker rooms at the same time, and he sees me in the hallway. And he told me I was 'a good nigger player.' That was progress in Texas, you know."

"Those guys were *really* racist," said Giers. "We almost got in a few big fights that game." So did Stangeland's dad, an imposing ex-police officer who shut up a row of Tyler fans in front of him who wouldn't stop spitting racist slurs.

Despite the clash of cultures and ways of living on the Rose Bowl field that day, Long Beach won. The Vikings' new coach was known for coming up with a gadget play every now and again, and he decided to use a unique one for an early kickoff return. "We'd practiced it in the last five minutes of every practice," Stangeland said. "But it never worked. We practiced it a hundred times and fumbled almost every time. We called it the fumblerooski play, and I said, 'If we ever have to use this, we're in trouble.'"

Instead, they ran it to perfection. Willie Martin fielded the ball but then threw it back to Dee Andrews, who proceeded to sprint eighty-five yards to pay dirt. In all, the play covered a hundred yards, which was a Junior Rose Bowl record that will never be broken. "Greatest play I was ever associated with," said Stangeland. "I remember our manager ran up to me and he said, 'Dee is lying in the end zone over there exhausted, and he's turning white.'"

That play rocked Tyler back on its heels, and the punishing Vikings backfield didn't let the Texas team dig its cleats in all game. As the Long Beach team pounded Tyler into the dirt, the Texans had to begrudgingly give the Vikings their due respect. "We put a whipping on them," said Andrews. "We showed them, if you're good, you're good. Japanese, white, black—we didn't care. We just played together. We weren't going to let anyone tear us apart, or tear our spirit down."

By the time the dust had settled, Long Beach had won 38–15, claiming its second national championship. Andrews was named Player of the Game for his incredible dash to the end zone on the opening kickoff, and the Vikings ended their first-ever undefeated season at 10–0, going down as one of the best teams in the history of Long Beach football.

1962 AND 1964 NATIONAL CHAMPIONS

After a brief pause to reload the talent chambers (many of the 1960 team went on to fantastic Division 1 careers after winning), the Vikings and Stangeland were right back at it in 1962. That year, they featured players such as Millikan's Gary Garrison and Poly stars Jeff Smith and Giers. Running back Homer Williams set the school's single-season record for rushing yards (1,267). He helped lead his team to a 6–0 start, beating Glendale 48–0 and easily dispatching New Mexico Military, Valley, San Diego, East Los Angeles, El Camino and Cerritos. Its 8–0 victory over Cerritos was the first time in Cerritos's history that the Falcons had been held scoreless.

Other than that game, the closest anyone had come to the Vikings was 24 points. Williams and quarterback Jimmy Dunn were powering

All-American Homer Williams in the 1962 Potato Bowl, which LBCC won for its third national title. *LBCC yearbook.*

an unstoppable offense, and the defense had allowed only 20 points in the Vikings' first six games. In their eighth, they once again rolled a shutout, their sixth of the year. Unfortunately, the Bakersfield defense did too, and the game ended 0–0, costing the Vikings a shot at the Junior Rose Bowl that year. They almost took a bigger hit when Bakersfield scored a touchdown after a referee had accidentally blocked Garrison, but the touchdown was called back due to a clipping penalty, preserving the scoreless tie.

After a 48–20 win over Santa Monica, the Vikings found themselves headed for the Potato Bowl, where they were to play Contra Costa. They knew they needed to put up a special performance if the pollsters were to name them co-national champions with the winner of that year's Junior Rose Bowl. And they did deliver. The Vikings beat Contra Costa 66–8, setting a new school record for most points scored. The crowd of 15,000 at the bowl game, held in Bakersfield, also set a record. Quarterback Ron

The scoreboard after the 1962 Potato Bowl, which may inspire a double-take. *LBCC yearbook.*

Richardson returned for the game, and Long Beach quickly found itself up 44–8, which had Stangeland pulling his starters, a move that barely slowed down the scoring.

It was a thorough enough victory that voters named them co-national champions with Santa Ana, which had triumphed in the Junior Rose Bowl. The next year was a down year for Stangeland's era as the Vikings went just 8–3, ending the season in a 48–15 drubbing of Mt. San Antonio College in the Elks Bowl. Williams was given conference player of the year honors, as the team improved its postseason bowl record to 5–0.

In 1964, Stangeland was happy to once again welcome in such Poly stars as Marvin Motley and Earl McCullouch, and the community once again rallied behind its homegrown superstars as they blew away the competition. The Vikings would outscore their opponents 348–88, in an undefeated 10–0 season that may be the single best in school history.

They started with a 45–0 victory over Santa Ana at Vets, a nice omen of things to come. Motley scored a seventy-four-yard touchdown, drubbing Fullerton 21–14 and setting up what was expected to be the showdown of all showdowns as the Vikings headed north to the Potato City, Bakersfield. The home team was undefeated and ranked number one in the nation. The game drew a crowd of over 18,000 to see its hometown team beat up the challengers from the South. But LBCC dashed those plans thanks to Motley's record ninety-six-yard touchdown. LBCC won, the final score being 27–6. Motley would go on to break Williams's rushing record by five yards.

The next week, the team managed a new school record with 577 yards, defeating Santa Monica 47–22. Quarterback Greg Barton passed for 337 yards and 5 touchdowns in the first half a few weeks later against East Los Angeles. It was looking more likely that Long Beach would have a shot at the Junior Rose Bowl, but it had to go undefeated. No matter how impressive their victories were, a single loss would force the Vikings into a lesser bowl game again.

There weren't many scares. The team's fans mostly spent their time rewriting the school records they found printed in their programs. Against Grossmont (a 47–0 win), Bob Stiles returned an interception ninety-seven yards for a touchdown, breaking the record Motley had set just a few weeks prior. The nail-biters came against Valley and El Camino. The latter was the season's homecoming game, played before nine thousand people at Vets, which saw the Vikings scoreless at halftime. But Motley ran in two touchdowns in the second half, and McCullouch polished off the 21–14 victory, showing the dazzling speed that made him "one of the fastest human beings alive," according to the school newspaper.

They played their final game on the road against Cerritos, with the Falcons looking to play spoiler before a rowdy crowd of 11,000. But Motley and McCullouch carried the day, and a 35–12 victory put Long Beach back in the Junior Rose Bowl where it belonged. Their opponent that year was to be an undefeated group from Cameron, Oklahoma. The Vikings had never lost in the annual contest between the nation's best junior college teams, but Cameron was a great squad, and the battle was expected to be fierce. A record crowd of 45,576 made its way to the Rose Bowl and could probably have been forgiven for asking for its money back.

Long Beach won 28–6. All-American lineman Fred Convertini and the rest of his group paved the way for a touchdown by fullback Elwood Stewart early in the game, and a forty-three-yard score by Motley, his seventeenth that year. Stiles returned an interception for a third score, and Barton tossed Ron Drake a thirty-two-yard score to cap the game and win a fourth national championship.

The 1964 LBCC team takes the field at the Junior Rose Bowl, where it would win its fourth national championship. *LBCC yearbook.*

At this point, Vikings fans felt they were on top of the world. The yearbook from the season refers to the team as fulfilling its "destiny" by winning the championship, one it was presumably supposed to fulfill year after year. And with a steady stream of Long Beach players coming in and a phenomenal motivator and tactician in Stangeland, why wouldn't fans expect to keep winning? The only thing that could have slowed the Vikings down was the Vikings.

But following that season, Stangeland decided to bring the Stangeland era at LBCC to an end. The job offers had finally grown too tempting, and he went to USC to be an assistant coach. He would spend four years as an assistant there before going on to become Long Beach State's most successful coach ever. But the Vikings wouldn't be the same without him. In fact, it would be three decades before they would even win a conference title again, much less a national one.

Several coaches tried their hand with the clipboard, some of them worthy (such as LBCC Hall of Famer Paul Chafe), but many of them not. Finally, after the 1991 season, athletic director Chuck McFerrin came to a decision and fired coach Wil Shaw after eight years that produced a 28–50–2 record. McFerrin told the *Los Angeles Times* that his next hire would represent a new beginning for the program and the school. "The community needed to believe that LBCC was serious about making a commitment, that football would be given the best opportunity to succeed here," McFerrin said. The job had long been held by part-timers—but McFerrin's hire, Larry Reisbig,

Running back Marvin Motley looks to the end zone in the '64 Junior Rose Bowl, behind his mammoth blockers. *LBCC yearbook.*

the former coach of Long Beach State and the secondary and special teams coach at Orange Coast College, signaled a change.

Sure enough, Reisbig brought a new focus and purpose to the team. The Vikings won conference championships in 1993 and 1994, his second and third years and, in 1993, were invited to their first postseason bowl game since 1965. They would win again in 1995, but a conference title isn't what that year is remembered for.

1995 NATIONAL CHAMPIONS

Reisbig brought the respect back to Long Beach City College, but in truth, there's probably no way in hell the 1995 team should have won a national championship. On October 21, the team was 6–0 and, perhaps overconfident, headed into a game with Palomar. At the start of the fourth quarter of that game, imagining they would finish undefeated was almost impossible: the Vikings trailed 45–17.

What followed was possibly the greatest comeback by any team in Long Beach history, given the odds, the time left on the clock and what was at stake. "I'm standing on the sideline thinking, 'Oh my God, it's our first loss,'" Reisbig recalled. "I'm trying to formulate what to say afterwards—right as I was doing that, we intercepted it and ran it into the end zone."

With less than eleven minutes remaining, quarterback Neo Aoga (another Poly product) began throwing seeds downfield. When the clock finally ticked down to 0:00, LBCC emerged victorious, 46–45. "After that game, the team believed that it could do anything," Reisbig told the *Los Angeles Times*. "Once we came back and won, things just started to mushroom for us." The comeback was so incredible that it actually ended with LBCC taking a knee, running the clock out instead of scoring another touchdown.

Aoga, receiver Jason McCorvey and running back Shawn Bane led a high-powered offense all year. Aoga, the "Throwin' Samoan," set (and still holds) most of the school's passing records and went 19–2 in his two years as a starter. That year, he was 206/384 for 3,626 yards and 37 touchdowns, while McCorvey hauled in 44 catches for 1,045 yards and 11 touchdowns, records for the school at the time. Bane added 1,171 yards and 11 touchdowns on the ground.

The Vikings played out the rest of their season undefeated and found themselves in the appetizingly titled Strawberry Bowl against Los Angeles Valley. Anyone who had been following the Vikings that season knew not to expect a defensive battle. Sure enough, over 100 points would be scored in the shootout, played at Cerritos College before 9,000. Aoga was behind much of the scoring, going 17/33 for 412 yards, and 3 touchdowns, adding another 2 on the ground. Long Beach won 59–49.

His offensive heroics and a defense that stopped Valley just enough times produced another LBCC win and another national championship, capping an 11–0 season. It was quite a turnaround for the Vikings, who had gone just 1–9 in 1991, the year before Reisbig took over. The whole

Head coach Larry Reisbig gives a pep talk to the 1995 Vikings, who would win their fifth national title. *LBCC yearbook.*

campus was booming, as the men's and women's track teams and the softball team also won state championships within twenty-four hours of the football game. Reisbig would go on to coach until 2002, winning five conference championships. When he stepped away, he did so as the winningest coach in the school's history, with a career record of 83–34–1.

Years later, Reisbig would tell a funny story about the secret forces at work in that ludicrous Palomar comeback:

> *In the newspaper, there were these dots, and it says if you rub the dots it will bring you luck. Well, after halftime, we're losing big, and my wife is sitting in the stands, she sees this paper in her purse—and she* [started] *rubbing the good luck dots. Sure enough, we got rolling, and everyone sitting around her wanted to rub them. She kept it after the game, so you know, that's the reason we won the national championship right there.*

Former Poly coach Jerry Jaso took the helm in 2003 for a five-year stint that saw the Vikings win two conference titles. Larry Reisbig's son, Mike, took the reins after that, starting his tenure in 2008. The team retains a distinctly

Long Beach flavor in its coaching staff; Aoga is one of many former players to return to the Vikings to coach. Of the eleven coaches with the team in 2011, seven of them played for Larry Reisbig.

Between the 1928 and 2011 seasons, the Long Beach City College Vikings won 405 games. They have seen a home stadium come up and school records come down with ease. They have sent 68 players to the NFL and 761 players on to four-year college ball. But, of course, the number they are best known for in Long Beach is the five national championships they brought to the city. And while it may feel like the years painted on the Vets press box have faded a bit in the seventeen seasons since its last national title, hope springs eternal at LBCC—after all, there's always room for more numbers on that box.

CHAPTER SEVEN

BEN AGAJANIAN

The Specialist

Although Ben Agajanian went to San Pedro High School, he was adopted as a Long Beach guy a long time ago, winning the Century Club Athlete of the Year award for the school in 1960 and 1968. Agajanian was certainly as good a free agent pickup as they come, and it doesn't hurt a city's football reputation to count the greatest kicker of all time among its ranks.

Agajanian had four toes on his kicking foot crushed in an elevator during college, an injury that, remarkably, had almost no impact on his career. He played at the University of New Mexico, and then "The Toeless Wonder" went on to kick professionally for twenty years (1945–64), one of just two players to play in the All-America Football Conference, the American Football League and the National Football League.

Among his many accomplishments, Agajanian can be said to have essentially invented the modern kicking game. The "soccer-style" of kicking bears his stamp, as do such innovations as the "three steps back, two steps over" technique, used by almost all NFL kickers today. He can also be credited with the development of modifications to the way that long snappers deliver the ball to the holder. His wildly different techniques and approach made him the NFL's first kicking specialist. In that era, field goal tries had been performed by players who already occupied other positions. But Agajanian was an asset everywhere he went, playing with ten different teams and winning championships with the 1956 Giants and the 1961 Packers.

Ben Agajanian working with tutee Ismael Ordonez, who went on to become a coach himself. *Courtesy* Press-Telegram.

He was such an authority that he also became the first-ever kicking coach in NFL history, coaching under Tom Landry with the Dallas Cowboys for twenty-four years and leading Landry to say, "He has done more for the kicking game in both college and the pros in the past fifty years than anybody I know."

For the last few decades, Agajanian has held a reputation for being a phenomenal teacher in Long Beach. His love of the kicking game was such that he hosted dozens of camps meant to help teach kids how to kick properly using his methods. He never charged a dime for the kicking/punting clinics, which are held in Long Beach's public parks and schools. In the time he was running the camps, over ten thousand local athletes cycled through to learn from a true master. Untold numbers of them went on to get college scholarships, creating a lasting legacy in football's most underappreciated discipline.

That lack of respect, sadly, has likely cost Agajanian a deserved spot in the Pro Football Hall of Fame. Canton has only three placekickers enshrined, and two of them played other positions. Agajanian's statistics and overall mark left on the game vastly outpaces those of the only "pure" kicker in the Hall of Fame, Jan Stenerud. Stenerud, however, was inducted over twenty years ago, and it seems unlikely that voters will ever recognize kickers in the future.

So perhaps Agajanian needed Long Beach as much as the city needed him. He is in the Long Beach Century Club Hall of Fame, after all.

CHAPTER EIGHT

St. Anthony

The Patron Saints of the Underdog

Long Beach isn't really known for a lot of underdog stories in the world of high school football; it's more of a Goliath town. But in the annals of Long Beach football history lies one of the great David stories of CIF football.

In 1921, when a tiny private Catholic school named St. Anthony opened, no one knew what was in the offing. At that time, it was relying on football equipment donated by the University of Notre Dame just to put clothes on its players. The Saints' first football teams in the late 1920s and early '30s were organized by a Mr. Henderson, a PE director at Franklin Junior High who would come to campus and organize after-school workouts. Orval McKee took over as a proper head coach in 1934, and the Saints quickly won their first game against one of the big public Long Beach schools, beating Jordan 12–0.

Clarence Layden, brother of Notre Dame great Elmer Layden, took over in 1936 and would lead the Saints to their first league championship in 1938 as they ran roughshod over the prep league competition (their closest game being a 28–0 victory). Mike Dimas was the coach when the gongs of war were ringing, and he left the school for World War II in 1941, making Brother Cyril, the school's athletic director, the temporary coach. Ernie Radford and Bud McKee were the next coaches, taking the school up to the 1945 season.

In 1946, an English teacher named Jacques Grenier took over head coaching duties. Grenier wasn't your usual coach. Bookish and incredibly bright, his previous coaching job was at Wilson High in Middletown,

"Johnny O" John Olszewski, the greatest Saint of all time. *Courtesy* Press-Telegram.

Connecticut, his home state. His backfield designs were so intricate that his best players, who moved on to California, would implement his plays mid-game when their collegiate offense was stalling. He was, in other words, the perfect underdog coach for a perfect underdog team. Over the next six years, he went 41–13–2, winning two league titles and a CIF shocker and retiring as the Saints coach with the highest winning percentage. No one since has bested his 73 percent record or won more league titles and, of course, no one since has come close to bringing the scrappy Saints the same championship thrill.

In Grenier's first season, the team finally found a home of its own at St. Anthony's Memorial Stadium (now Clark Field), just in time for the Saints to go 5–2–1 and take second place in the Catholic League. Grenier was busy, coaching basketball and baseball at the school as well. In 1947, they won their first Catholic League title and featured a running back by the name of John Olszewski, who became the first Saint in history to be named to the All-CIF list and the first to be named first-team All-City in Long Beach. With a number of great players returning, including "Johnny O," the stage was set for a magical year.

1948: David vs. Goliaths

Bob Keisser of the *Press-Telegram*, in his excellent retrospective on the team, wrote:

> *The Saints of '48 were the last true underdog to win a CIF major division title, a small Catholic school with around 300 students and 32 players on its varsity beating public school behemoths San Diego, Chaffey and Santa Barbara to win the title.*

Keep in mind that in 1948, there weren't multiple divisions the way there are now: every team in Southern California competed for one single trophy. And the Saints, outmanned by a hundred players on their football team and three thousand heads in their student body, not only competed but won.

The backfield was made up of a platoon of studs called the "Golden Saints" of St. Anthony, so named because all four of them would earn scholarships to play for the Golden Bears. The physically punishing Johnny O led a three-headed monster of running backs, along with scat-back John

Peterson and fullback Dean O'Hare. Quarterback Bill Mais was tasked with keeping Grenier's offense humming. That wasn't a problem. The team beat Newport Harbor, Cathedral, Compton, Downey, Burroughs, St. Monica, Loyola and St. Augustine. Its only loss was in a rematch with Mt. Carmel, 14–13. Of those schools, only St. Monica had a smaller graduating class than the Saints.

Olszewski piled up yardage, rushing for 1,662 yards and 27 touchdowns that year alone, while splitting time with two other Division 1 backs. He made the most of each carry, averaging over 11 yards each time he took the ball. In the playoffs, the Saints opened with a 28–20 win over public school juggernaut San Diego, and then edged Chaffey on the road, 28–21. The *Independent*'s phone lines were described as being "ablaze," as Long Beach residents called the newspaper all night to try and find out the results of the away game. Grenier had come up with an idea for a new play a few days prior to the game and scratched it out in the dirt for Olszewski, who executed it so perfectly that three of the team's four touchdowns came off that one motion. Olszewski, of course, also scored the fourth touchdown as well. On the day, he had touchdowns of 79, 64, 41 and 22 yards. But the game and the season took a toll on Johnny O, and he would only spend a few minutes on the field the next week.

The Saints were to face yet another team expected to overpower them, Santa Barbara, in the CIF championship game at the Coliseum that year. After the game, a bright future spread itself out before Johnny O, who would be named the CIF and the state Player of the Year (the only Saint to earn either honor, ever) and All-American and who would go on to a successful career at Cal before being drafted fourth overall in the NFL. He spent a decade in the pros, earning the first of two NFL Pro Bowl nods in his rookie year. The St. Anthony football record book is dedicated to him, calling him, "Indisputably the most legendary football player ever to play at St. Anthony." Johnny O was so good that all these things happening in the future actually seemed plausible at the time. But he was to sit on the bench for almost the entire game against Santa Barbara. How could David stand his ground against yet another Goliath?

Well, for starters, the other Saints were pretty damn good. But there was also a brotherhood among them that simply wouldn't allow them to lose. Olszewski, Peterson, Mais and O'Hare had grown up playing together, spent all their time hanging out together and didn't choose to attend the same college on accident. According to Keisser's column, Peterson and O'Hare even lived together for a few years, when O'Hare's father, a navy

John Peterson, one of the "Golden Saints." *Courtesy* Press-Telegram.

commander, was assigned to China. After their playing days were done, all four would return to Long Beach and would remain close friends for life. The whole team rallied in the title game against Santa Barbara. And if it couldn't win, it could at least figure a way not to lose.

Mais threw a thirty-two-yard strike to Mike Hendren, St. Anthony's only score the entire game. Santa Barbara also scored in the first half, though, and the game went to halftime tied. It would end the same way, thanks to the defensive heroics of O'Hare and the rest of the Saints. Like David in the dusty circle with Goliath, their focus had to be immaculate—one long run for a score or to set up a field goal would have snatched immortality from the Saints. But they guarded their end perfectly, and regulation ended in a 7–7 tie. The tiebreaker at the time wasn't overtime, but first downs, and St. Anthony won 16–12, giving the Saints sole possession of the CIF championship.

For one brief moment, the players' brotherhood actually hurt them. Olszewski had seen a weakness in Santa Barbara and excitedly hurried onto the field to tell his teammates, but he did so before the referee had officially called a play over, earning a penalty that awarded one of Santa Barbara's twelve first downs. Santa Barbara actually had more first downs at halftime, but Mais led several long, nonscoring drives in the second half to put his team ahead.

When a reporter asked Grenier what made his team tick and how it had managed to pull off such a string of upsets, he shrugged the question off: "Well, I think it is the morale of the boys, the unselfishness of every boy, including Olszewski. They are all out there to win without thinking of personal glory." By winning, of course, the Saints earned more glory for themselves and their school than any players before or since. Grenier himself, always an odd duck for a football coach, went on to fame (if not fortune) as a harness racer, a sport he excelled at as a professional from 1952–68, winning 733 races and earning himself a spot in the sport's Hall of Fame.

The quartet of backfield stars was much sought after, as Mais recalled: "We were all recruited by USC. But Cal had just played in the Rose Bowl and Pappy Waldorf was the coach. UCLA's Red Sanders was really hot after Dean, telling him he wanted him to run his single wing as a blocking quarterback and telling Dean he'd be an All-American."

But Grenier had several ties with Cal, and one of the team's assistants, Johnny Graves, was a Long Beach guy. Johnny O was the first to commit. Once he did, his three friends followed almost immediately. After their

Coach Jacques Grenier, who won the only CIF title at St. Anthony, shown here during his later successful career in harness racing. *Courtesy* Press-Telegram.

St. Anthony's CIF title team in 1948, one of the great David v. Goliath stories in CIF history. *St. Anthony yearbook.*

stellar college and pro careers had ended, they rose to prominence in their hometown, Olszewski earning fame as the head of Long Beach's famed lifeguards program. Peterson became the city attorney, while O'Hare was named Century Club president in 1961.

Mais told Keisser, "We were all very, very lucky to have spent so many years together. I really have no idea how everyone came together, but once we did, we stayed together. We sort of knew back then that it was special, and all these years later, it still is."

A special brotherhood, a special team—one for the ages. The Saints proved once and for all that even in football, where the outmuscled so rarely hoist a trophy, one strong David is worth a half-dozen Goliaths.

Grenier's other teams were all competitive, as were those of Ennio Arboit, who took over after Grenier and led the team to win league titles in 1952 and '53. Arboit was using many of Grenier's plays and designs, so the Frenchman can certainly be credited with some of the team's inspiration, but great players like receiver George Sherwood and tiny running back Dick Romo certainly helped. Romo remains a top-five career leader in most rushing categories for the Saints. Arboit and Grenier are the only coaches in the school's history to win multiple league titles.

Since 1980, the school has won only four of them and has more often resembled the underfunded, undermanned program expected from a school of St. Anthony's size, especially since budgets around Southern California have soared. The titles were won by coaches who were usually on their way up or down from jobs at the city's other, larger schools. Mike Reisbig won one in 1987, many years before he would take over as head coach of the

LBCC Vikings, and Dave Radford won one in 1991, just a year after being fired from the head job at Millikan. The most recent league title was won in 1999 by Jeff Turley, whose next job as defensive coordinator on four of Poly's CIF championship teams would bring him much more acclaim.

But while the team was often short of the talent needed to make waves in the modern CIF, the Saints have boasted some big, big names. In 1960, a lineman by the name of Jack Snow starred in his senior year for the Saints, earning All-State honors. Snow lettered ten times at St. Anthony, believed to be the most of any athlete ever. He excelled in football, basketball and baseball and, after phenomenal play on the football team during his senior year, he hit .458 on the baseball team and earned All-City honors. His gridiron skills earned him a scholarship to Notre Dame, perhaps St. Anthony's way of paying the Fighting Irish back for their equipment loan in the late '20s. While there, Snow was named an All-American as a receiver in 1964, with the high point of his season coming against Wisconsin, when he racked up 276 yards—still good for the third-highest single-game total in the school's illustrious history. That year he finished fifth in Heisman voting.

Snow was drafted eighth overall by the Vikings in 1965 but was traded to the Rams, where he spent a decade as a star receiver, which included an NFL Pro Bowl trip in 1967. After retiring, Snow was the longtime host of the Rams' radio program, following them to St. Louis when the team moved out of Los Angeles. Meanwhile, his son, J.T., was starring at nearby Los Alamitos High and then going on to a long, prosperous baseball career with the San Francisco Giants. When Jack passed away in 2005, J.T. donned his football number, 84, and wore it in honor of his father.

Cormac Carney was a wide receiver at St. Anthony, where he was named two-time All-City player. But off the football field, he snared what must be one of the strangest post-football careers imaginable. After starring as a Saint, Carney went to UCLA to play wide receiver, leading the team in receiving each year he was a Bruin while maintaining a 3.5 GPA in psychology. Among his accomplishments as a Bruin, Carney was twice named All-Conference and academic All-American, and he helped lead the team to its signature 1983 Rose Bowl victory over Michigan.

After football, Carney went to law school and then went into private practice. In 2001, he was appointed to the California Superior Court in Orange County and then, in 2003, he became the first and only Long Beach football player to become a federal judge when he was appointed by President George W. Bush to a United States District Court for the Central District of California seat.

Cormac Carney, a star wide receiver for the Saints who went on to play at UCLA and eventually became a federal judge. *Publicity photo.*

In 1987, quarterback Dan O'Shea would finish his career by proving himself the best statistical signal-caller in school history. He was named Long Beach City Player of the Year and All-CIF and had a phenomenal year overall. O'Shea has two of the best four seasons in school history in passing yardage and ten more touchdown passes than the number two player. Along with the four Golden Saints and running back Dwayne Faciane, O'Shea is the sixth Saint in school history to have his jersey retired.

After assistant coaching stints under Dave Radford and at Wilson and St. John Bosco, O'Shea took a crack at being the head coach at his alma mater. But at a St. Anthony struggling to find its place in the new CIF, his teams went 3–16–1 in 2003 and 2004. Still, the league title he and coach Reisbig brought the school is memorable, partially because the Saints have only won three since.

In 1993, Radford began a series with the St. Mary's Saints, a private school team in Canada. The games would come to be known as the Saint Bowl, and the teams took turns traveling to play each other across the border, with the visiting team having to learn its host's rules for that contest. The

Dan O'Shea, the greatest quaterback in Saints history. *St. Anthony yearbook.*

series carried on each year from 1993–2000, before the travel complications following September 11 halted it. But athletic director Brian Walsh revived it in 2011, and St. Anthony hosted and lost the game.

The Saints are a school with a long and proud tradition. The world of high school football has grown larger, while the campus and student body at St. Anthony have not, and the school remains an education-first Catholic school, unlike the Mater Deis and other Catholic powers with six-figure budgets. But as the Saints themselves proved in 1948, Goliaths can grow all they want—David will always have a shot.

CHAPTER NINE

Pro Football in Long Beach

John Dixon, former sports editor of the *Press-Telegram*, carved the gravestone of professional sports in Long Beach with this sentence in his "Long Beach Sports History" piece: "Few American cities can rival the accomplishments of Long Beach's youth, but few cities have such a chronicle of non-support of professional franchises."

In these pages, you've already read about the dozens of games with ten thousand or more fans in attendance for high school football games. Poly's Moore League clash with Lakewood, dubbed the Moore League Super Bowl, has drawn better than that number each of the last six years, a remarkable number for a prep game. But the prep game has always been Long Beach's fascination—the shoulders of the 710 freeways are lined with the carcasses of cast-off pro sports teams.

More recently, the Armada baseball team and the Ice Dogs hockey team have been casualties of Long Beach's noninterest in pro sports teams bearing its name. But going back through the football record books is a depressing experience. Here's an incomplete listing of some of the teams that have tried to catch on here: the Quake, the Breakers, the Aftershock, the Muscle Heads, the Lions, the Mustangs, the Bulldogs and the All-Americans.

Interestingly, Long Beach's forward-thinking attitudes about women in sports opened the road for four separate women's football teams, although the city's citizens didn't buy enough tickets to support them. The first, the Dandelions, was founded in 1975 and outlasted the Quake and the Breakers.

More recently, the Aftershock made it from 2003–2005 at Vets before folding. It is believed that no city has had more women's professional football teams call it home than Long Beach—of course, that also means no city has seen more professional women's teams fail than Long Beach.

The men haven't fared much better. There were the Long Beach Muscle Heads, a National Indoor Football League team scheduled to start in 2007. Several press releases were sent to local media, but the team had vanished by the time the league's schedule was released. The Long Beach Admirals were established at Vets on August 1, 1967. They would play their final game four weeks later.

There is some history there, however. The Long Beach Bulldogs were the first pro team to inhabit Vets, a team that had formerly been based in Los Angeles but wanted a more "local" town to call home (meaning a town where they didn't have to compete with the Rams). Poly star Willie Martin played for the Long Beach Falcons in the 1960s, a team run by Long Beach great Ben Agajanian for a time. And the Long Beach Mustangs gave it a go in the 1970s, surviving for a few years before folding.

There is something about the city's sense of community that keeps convincing people to try again. Even today, two teams are scheduled to use Vets as their home base for 2012: the Beach Cities All-Americans, and the Long Beach Lions (adding to the already impressive menagerie of Falcons, Mustangs, Bulldogs, Admirals, and whatever Muscle Heads are meant to represent).

One pro team that had no trouble thriving in Long Beach, however, was the Los Angeles Rams. The Rams didn't play in Long Beach but did use Blair Field (the baseball stadium in Recreation Park) as the site of their training camp for thirteen years in the late 1960s and '70s. The team had considered using Wilson High and the facilities at the navy base on Terminal Island in 1950 but had opted for a different location, only to return a few decades later. That led to some interesting stories, particularly when the team was coached by future Hall of Famer George Allen. Allen was notoriously private and actually ordered the windows on the east side of Wilson High (which faced the field) shuttered while the team was practicing.

So the only pro team the city might have been interested in was practicing daily at Blair Field, but Long Beach residents weren't allowed to watch. *Press-Telegram* sports editor Jim McCormick had a solution, sending a photographer up into the eucalyptus trees that overlooked the outfield wall early in the morning, and then printing the covert shots in the next day's paper. Allen was not thrilled.

Tom Nordee, the "King of Sandlot Football," who never played high school ball but won a number of semi-pro titles. *Courtesy* Press-Telegram.

Though not professional, another team unassociated with a school called Long Beach home. The Terminal Island Islanders were a team made up of naval officers who would do the "service football" circuit, usually playing teams from other bases in the area but occasionally taking on college or junior college teams. For a time after World War II, service football was very popular on the West Coast, and the Islanders made an impression.

The Islanders lost a close game with Pepperdine one year but won a pair against UCLA in the next few years. The facilities on Terminal Island played neutral host to a game between Camp Pendleton (featuring Long Beach native Bob Hodal) and the Hawaii Packers, who lost to Pendleton 68–0. That put the Pendleton squad into a game against the Rams in San Diego for a naval relief fundraiser. Hodal would lead his team to the All-Navy Football championship, where it lost to Quantico 14–13 in a game played at the Coliseum.

Because of the high sense of patriotism and the presence of local players, the service football Islanders were able to develop a little following. Owners who have tried and failed to plant a team in Long Beach are probably slapping themselves. All they needed was a roster full of native Long Beach World War II veterans, and perhaps their team could have gotten off the ground. Since that's never going to happen, it's more likely that, as Poly and Wilson and the other schools roll on, more pro teams will try and fail.

CHAPTER TEN

Long Beach State

The Paradoxical 49ers

The campus of Long Beach State is a sprawling, teeming thing. Built on the city's second largest hill, with over 35,000 students and faculty, it's always busy and always moving. If you walk around the quad or the food court on a Tuesday afternoon, you'll see one shirt over and over again. It's oxford grey and reads "Long Beach State" at the top. In the center is a football emblazoned with the familiar "LB" logo. And on the bottom row, it says, "Undefeated since 1991."

The joke, of course, is that the school hasn't had a team since 1991—a fact that hasn't kept the $16.95 tee shirt mocking that fact from flying off the shelves of the campus bookstore. Like most things surrounding the school's pigskin history, the shirt is a paradox. Since the football team was shut down over twenty years ago, the school has won three national championships, one in men's volleyball and two in women's volleyball. The Dirtbags baseball team has gone to the College World Series twice. The men's basketball team has made the NCAA Tournament four times, and the women's soccer team three times, including an Elite Eight run in 2011.

Still, ask a bookstore employee what its top-selling piece of gear is in the last five years, and he won't even hesitate: "The football shirt." It's a fitting oddity for a school whose only bowl game appearance ended in a tie, whose most famous coach was rumored to have died as a result of celebrating not a national championship but finishing over .500.

The pride in Long Beach State's football team still runs high. The football 49ers are literally how the school got its colors and are still the only football team in Long Beach to have retired every single jersey number.

THE EARLY YEARS

The 49ers first donned their brown and gold uniforms in 1955, under head coach Mike DeLotto, who ran the team for their first three years of existence. Their first game was a 21–6 loss to Occidental that fall, but the 49ers quickly evened their season and all-time record at .500 with a 28–12 victory over LaVerne. DeLotto's 49ers went 5–2 in their first season, playing as an independent team unattached to a conference. The next year, he guided them to a 5–3 record, including wins over Pepperdine and UC Davis and losses to future league-mates UC Santa Barbara and Cal Poly.

The wheels came off the wagon for DeLotto and his crew in 1957, though, as they stumbled to a 3–5 record, the first losing campaign the school had experienced. Change was on the horizon. It was time to join a conference, leave "independent" status behind and find a new coach.

The next year, Don Reed piloted the 49ers as they joined the California Collegiate Athletic Association (CCAA). Reed never won a conference title but would coach the team from 1958–68, compiling a 57–47–2 record. After spending his first two years getting the team on track, he did not suffer another losing campaign until his final season as the team's coach.

Reed was considered a brilliant offensive mind, and he remained a consultant for future coaches looking to pick his brain. Other than Jim Stangeland, who would bring the school to the greatest success it had ever seen, Reed is the only coach to be inducted into the Long Beach State (LBSU) Hall of Fame. His first year as coach, he watched lineman Carl Evans graduate. The former Jordan Panther, also a member of the LBSU Hall of Fame, was the 49ers' first four-year letterman.

One newspaper wryly noted that, while the 49ers did finish their '58 season at the Rose Bowl against Cal State LA, the only thing riding on that game was which team would finish slightly further from last place. The game ended in a 6–6 tie, as the 49ers finished Reed's first year 2–6–1. The next two years, they went 4–5, and then 5–3–1 as Reed and his players turned the team around. Dallas Moon was the team's quarterback, still years away from his tragic death in a plane crash at the age of thirty. He and fellow future Hall of Famer Dick Keelor led the team in turning around the culture and competing against the CCAA competition.

The peak of the Reed era came in 1964 and '65, when the team finished 8–2 and 9–1. It never claimed a CCAA title, thanks to losses to Cal State LA both seasons, but the profile of the program was raised considerably. The 49ers broke thirty individual and team records and achieved their first-ever

Dee Andrews, a mid-1960s star at Long Beach State in football and track. *Courtesy Long Beach State.*

national ranking. Reed developed a reputation as a coach willing to adjust his system to his players. In 1964, that meant running the ball, as former Poly and LBCC star Dee Andrews broke the school's single-game and career rushing records.

Andrews was coached by backfield assistant Stu Farber, who had been an All-City quarterback at Poly and who had won a national championship with LBCC in 1950. Andrews, a Hall of Famer at the school, was one of the fastest athletes the university would ever see, and when football season was finished, he would move to track, where he set school records in the long jump and the high hurdles.

In 1965, Reed returned seventeen lettermen from the 8–2 previous season. The 49ers were able to shift back to passing the ball more after Andrews graduated, and they lit up the scoreboard. They averaged 32 points per game and scored fewer than 27 points just twice in a 14–12 nail-biter against Fresno State. Their only blemish that year was a 27–21 defeat to CSULA.

The future felt wide open at the school. The media guide noted, "Football is on the upswing," and it was hard not to agree. Lynn Hoyem, a high school quarterback who had become an interior lineman at Long Beach State, became the school's first player drafted into the NFL, enjoying a six-year pro career. (He would, tragically, also later die in a plane crash.)

But the Reed era had already reached its peak. In the next three years, the school went 6–3, 5–5 and 3–7, despite having All-American receiver Billy Parks on the team that third year. High expectations for 1968 were met with the school's first losing season in a decade, and Long Beach State looked around for the coach who could take them to the next level. The man they found was already a well-known coach in the city.

THE STANGELAND YEARS

Jim Stangeland blew onto campus like a stiff ocean breeze. The disciplinarian, nicknamed "The Colonel," had been an air force pilot in his precoaching life. But it was his eight-year, three-time national championship stint at Long Beach City College that locals knew him for. He had left the Vikings after his third national title in 1964 to be an assistant coach at USC for four years. There, he coached a backfield that featured Mike Garrett and O.J. Simpson and won a national championship. But he

Jim Stangeland, already a name in the city because of his three national titles at LBCC, would win two of the 49ers' three conference titles and take them to their only bowl appearance. *Courtesy Long Beach State.*

returned to Long Beach, the city he made his name in, because he believed he could win at Long Beach State.

"Long Beach was like a sleeping giant to me," he would tell the *Los Angeles Times* decades after he left. Stangeland was just the man to wake it up. In 1969, his 49ers went 8–3, as a talented roster developed under his grueling practices. Dee Andrews was back as an assistant coach, while serving as the athletic director at Franklin Junior High, and the team had a distinctly Long Beach flavor; one of the motives behind hiring Stangeland was his ability to bring in top Long Beach talent.

The football team joined the Pacific Coast Athletic Association that year (it would later become the Big West, the conference the school's other sports still belong to). The only losses in 1969 were to Texas A&I, California State at Northridge and a season-finale defeat at the hands of the San Diego State Aztecs that would haunt the team's offseason. The Aztecs hadn't lost in two years, but the 49ers led by nine points at halftime and were clinging to a small lead with three seconds left. San Diego State's pass-happy coach, Don Coryell (who would redefine the pro passing game with the Chargers later in life), was hoping for a miracle when he called a downfield bomb, and he got it in the form of a defensive pass interference call. The Aztecs scored on the next play and beat the 49ers 36–32.

"So my senior year, we were ready for those guys," said Jeff Severson, a Hall of Fame defensive back for the 49ers who went on to an eight-year NFL career. "Oh yeah, we were ready."

1970: Bowl Bound

The 1970 season looked like a movie script for the 49ers—so much so, in fact, that cornerback Jeff Severson actually wrote a screenplay treatment based on that year. The team had returning talent by the bucket load. Severson had set an NCAA record for single-season interceptions in 1969 (fourteen) that still stands today. Running back Leon Burns was the nation's leading rusher and scorer in 1969 and was a legitimate star in the world of NCAA football that year.

Seven years prior, when Burns was arrested as an accessory to theft, you would never have known it. In Long Beach, Burns was known as a sweet-hearted competitor, but his past was troubled. He'd grown up in Oakland and had been arrested just out of high school after his friends were found dividing up stolen goods in his house. He would spend five years in prison, doing nothing but lifting weights, shoveling dung (his assigned duty) and playing football. It was at an intramural prison game that the head coach of Laney Junior College noticed him and told him to give him a call when he got out. According to Severson, the other player the coach wanted (a tall, blonde quarterback) had to decline (he was in jail for life for murdering his wife and her boyfriend).

When Burns got out, he mowed through the junior college competition. It wasn't even fair. And when he got down to Long Beach State, it was the same story. Burns was just over six feet tall, bench pressed 450 pounds and ran a 4.4 40. He was a nearly unprecedented combination of strength and speed. *Press-Telegram* sports editor Hank Hollingworth wrote, "Outside of Jim Brown, he's the finest running back I've ever seen in college football."

He proved it in '69 as the nation's top running back, piling up 1,659 yards and 27 touchdowns. In the 1970 media guide, his picture not only appears

Leon Burns, All-American running back, performing one of his signature overhead lifts. *Courtesy Long Beach State.*

on the cover, but Burns actually got his own section of the book. The *Press-Telegram*'s Jim McCormick photographed Burns holding his blocking fullback, Hans Albrecht, over his head like a trophy, and the theme caught on. Photos exist of Burns hoisting water coolers, cheerleaders and benches over his head.

"He was like a damn Adonis," said McCormick. "The photo was his suggestion, too."

A bumper sticker with Burns lifting Albrecht with the text, "Have you seen Leon?" was printed and quickly became a fad.

Fans had, in fact, seen Leon, and they knew that what he was carrying in 1970 was the team's fortunes. Stangeland convened training camp at the Terminal Island Naval Base that year, housing his team in the barracks and holding four two-hour practices a day, with a dawn run and a mile-long night run sandwiching that grinding schedule. "It was like the Junction Boys," recalled Severson. "I mean, we had people disappearing at night because they couldn't handle it."

Even Dave Radford, a defensive backs coach on the team, agreed. "Gitmo couldn't be any tougher," he said.

The intense training paid off. The 49ers weren't a deep roster thanks to the midnight defections (Severson said there were two backups for the entire defensive backfield), but the players who stuck with Stangeland through his workouts were ferocious. The team defeated Montana State and then suffered defeats to Pacific (by a score of 9–6) and Hawaii (23–14). It wouldn't lose another game all year, making it the last time in school history it had fewer than three losses. Defensive lineman John Kahler, a recent Hall of Fame inductee at the school, developed a reputation as a fierce competitor.

They beat San Jose State, Boise State, Santa Barbara, California Polytechnic, Fresno State and CSULA. Coaches usually encourage their teams to "take it one game at a time," but there was no doubt that the entire 49er roster was waiting to meet at Anaheim Stadium on November 20. That was when the 49ers and Aztecs were to meet again, a fiery rematch on the home field of the California Angels.

The Aztecs were a cocky bunch, and they had reason to be. Coryell's San Diego State team hadn't lost a game in thirty-two tries and was ranked in the top ten nationally, ahead of UCLA and USC. It was the king of Southern California and was taking the field against a team that, although somewhat improved, had more often played the role of court jester than title contender.

The storylines were rich: over 39,000 fans crammed into the stadium (the previous record for home attendance for a 49ers game was 18,000). The San Diego State side was already chanting, "Bring on Ohio State," as fans expected to see the Buckeyes in a bowl game at the end of the year. "The greatest fight speech anyone ever gave our team," remembered a grinning Stangeland. Instead, Long Beach State beat the pants off them. The final score was 27–11, and it wasn't even that close.

"It was decisive," said Severson, still pleased with the win forty-two years later. "We clobbered them." Stangeland's brilliant move was to run a lot of fakes to Burns, whom he knew the Aztecs would load up on. The 49ers' best player (perhaps of all time) served as a perfect decoy, while the team ran spin plays and counters with Albrecht. Brian Shaw, the other corner for the 49ers, was the little brother of the Aztecs quarterback, which Radford said was an advantage.

Angel Stadium. This is where the 49ers played their home games for a number of years. *Courtesy Long Beach State.*

"Brian's dad said that at home when they played checkers or marbles, Brian always won. Jeff also only had six interceptions that year because nobody would throw at him (after he set the NCAA record in 1969). But that day he had three picks."

After the game, the Long Beach State fans poured out of the stands, flooding the field. Burns took off his shoulder pads and, surrounded by fans, he ripped his jersey open, revealing a Superman shirt underneath. The students and boosters ate it up. It was a sweet celebration and probably the biggest win in the school's football history.

"The whole season was predicated on that," said Severson. "That's really what our whole goal was, and it was mayhem on that field." Not only had the 49ers shocked the Aztecs, they had clinched their first-ever conference title.

"It really put Long Beach on the map," said McCormick. "It was easily their best football victory ever."

The program cover for the 49ers' 1970 victory over San Diego State, considered the most important win in school history. *Courtesy Long Beach State.*

To end the season, the team traveled to Pasadena for the Pasadena Bowl, playing against Louisville, a team coached by Lee Corso and captained by Tom Jackson. Severson refers to that game as "the icing on the cake" of a memorable season.

Louisville was as happy to see the 49ers as the 49ers were to see them. "Let me say one thing," Corso (never short on commentary) told the Pasadena Quarterback Club before the game. "I'm sure glad Long Beach shut that San Diego State bunch up."

But in the game, it was obvious that the 49ers had already achieved their goal for the year. They fell behind 14–7 after the first quarter, and had to play from behind, set back by two goal-line fumbles. But the 49ers did battle back, as the defense only gave up three points in the second half, producing a safety as well. When Burns scored a touchdown and the team completed a two-point conversion with 1:55 left in the fourth quarter, the game was tied at 24. Louisville had a chance to win it on a field goal, but the 49ers had Severson. "I'd been setting their guy up by running outside all game, so I faked that way and cut in on him, then laid out," he remembered. He blocked the kick (the only kick Louisville's kicker ever missed in college), keeping the game in a deadlock. Stangeland made a key protest as well.

"They threw a double pass into the end zone, but the lateral was forward. The officials didn't see it, but I saw it. After it was over I ran out and yelled, 'Two forward passes!' The officials talked and agreed it had been, and they called it back and penalized them. And the game was over." The official box score is approved by a familiar name: Jim Lineberger, a former Poly player and Wilson coach and Severson's coach at Jefferson Junior High.

It was the cap to a fantastic year, one in which the Superman, Burns, had led the 49ers to a 2,619-yard tally on the ground. That summer, he would become one of just two first-round draft picks in school history and the highest pick ever at thirteenth overall. But Burns's flame had burned out. Injuries cut his career short, and he was shot to death in December 1985, a murder that remains unsolved.

The 49ers had peaked, too. Stangeland's group defended its conference championship in 1971 but were just 8–4 and did not receive a postseason bowl bid. Things were rapidly coming undone, and the team went 5–6 the next year and 1–9 the year after that, the worst year in school history and Stangeland's last. "Many people coach too long," he told the *Los Angeles Times*, "and I did."

The Fall

But things weren't going to be that simple. On January 1, 1974, Stangeland announced his retirement. Five days later, at its conference in San Francisco, the NCAA announced the results of a multiyear sweeping investigation into numerous violations by the 49ers' football and basketball teams. Players, including Burns, were alleged to have been given rent money, jobs and other illegal benefits. Both teams were placed on probation for three years as a result.

There was an emotional outpour in Long Beach. A banner reading, THE NCAA IS A FOUR LETTER WORD was hung, and fans and coaches alike pointed their finger at UCLA and USC, a pair of huge schools competing in the same market, widely known among insiders to have committed much worse sins than the lowly 49ers, who were scraping by on almost no money. "The NCAA coming into Long Beach on its witch hunt," Stangeland told *Sports Illustrated* in a large exposé on the findings, "is like the United Nations marching on Poland for not fighting fair against Germany in World War II."

Then, and in later years, Stangeland would appear to be at peace with what his program had been found doing. A feature in *Sports Illustrated* read: "When Stangeland discovered that a standout running back was living in the back seat of a car, he directed the player to a booster who rented the player a flat at a bargain price. Another time, he gave an old blazer to a player who needed one."

"Technically [according to NCAA rules], you can't do that," Stangeland said. "But I'm not made that way. So I'm going to help that kid."

There is an old joke among NCAA mid-majors regarding the organization's preferential treatment to its larger members. The names of the schools are interchangeable but, in the mid-70s, it would have gone, "The NCAA was so mad at UCLA that it put Long Beach State on probation." *Sports Illustrated* summed up the views of many locals by saying, "Many people viewed the NCAA sanctions as punishment for a university that grew too successful too fast."

It was certainly curious that the NCAA put two of its four full-time investigators on the school for over a year, interviewing people (according to *Sports Illustrated*) in Long Beach, New York, Detroit, San Francisco, Phoenix, St. Louis, Las Vegas, New Jersey, Mississippi, Michigan and even the Los Angeles County Jail. Regardless of how you see the morality of a little school using big school tactics to compete with big schools, the result of the sentencing was clear: it brought Long Beach State to its knees. And the football team would take a long time getting back up.

Waiting for Elvis

Four men coached the 49ers from 1974–89: Wayne Howard, Dave Currey, Mike Sheppard and Larry Reisbig. They won a conference title, their third and final one, in 1980, under Currey, with an 8–3 record. In 1978, the San Francisco 49ers took linebacker Dan Bunz with the twenty-fourth overall pick in the draft, making Bunz the school's second (and final) first-round draft pick, after Burns. Bunz played in the NFL for eight years, including seven with the 49ers. In Super Bowl XVI, the first of two rings he would win with the 49ers, Bunz made "the Stop," a play that lives on in Super Bowl lore; he grabbed receiver Charles Alexander by the waist just before the goal line and flung him backward, keeping the Bengals out of the end zone. If he had not made the tackle, the 49ers wouldn't have won their first Super Bowl.

In 1986, the wolves were at the program's door, as the school began to discuss shutting down the football team. Larry Reisbig, who would go on to win a national championship at Long Beach City College, kept the program afloat by raising $315,000 in a matter of months, with the help of the Century Club and other community groups. But the wolves would be back. After the 1989 season, Reisbig was told he could either resign or be fired, and he chose to resign. He was disappointed not to be able to see out the next season.

"That's what we'd been waiting for. We redshirted nine guys waiting for that fourth year," he said. "And we actually were going to have six or seven games at home for the first time. We had been playing all but four of our games on the road each year, just trying to make enough money to keep going."

Stangeland's description of the school as a "sleeping giant" seemed apt. The 49ers had some success and had some players drafted, but there was always the sense that things could get much better. After all, the student population was bigger in Long Beach than at UCLA or USC, and the school was located in one of the nation's best recruiting hotbeds; there was gunpowder there. It just needed a spark. But what came in 1990 wasn't a spark so much as a flamethrower.

George Allen: The Future Is Now

There is simply no way to accurately describe the absurdity of the media circus that surrounded the university's next hire. George Allen was in the Pro Football Hall of Fame for the wonders he worked—with the Rams, Redskins, and Bears—and he never once coached a losing season in his twenty-one years in the league. He had been out of the NFL since 1977, his legacy intact, and he spent his retirement hanging out with celebrities and running a Ronald Reagan–sponsored national campaign to help keep high school students in shape.

"They were interviewing everyone at the Holiday Inn, the head coach of El Camino, an assistant from USC, all those guys," said Bill Brady, an assistant athletic director at Long Beach State and a quarterback on Allen's team. "And then they get a call (from the guy in charge of finding a coach) that says, 'We've got one more candidate.' And when they went to the Marriott, to the Presidential Suite, it was George Allen."

After a quick negotiation (Allen asked for things the university said yes to), Long Beach State, the shy kid in the corner of the dance, suddenly found itself waltzing with Miss Universe. Nobody could understand what was happening. Even *Sports Illustrated* asked, "Why, George?" The subheadline of that article read, "At 72, George Allen has decided to coach a dismal college team." The *New York Times*' headline read, "Allen's Return to Coaching Is Painful." But Allen said he relished the challenge, and onto the campus he blew, like a tornado. His wife, Ettie, wept when she saw his office. Allen probably wept inwardly when he saw the level of players at his disposal.

Perhaps nobody was more shocked than Reisbig, though. After all, just a few years prior, he had raised over $300,000 just to keep the doors open. Now, a few months later, the school hired a six-figure superstar. "It hit me like a bombshell," he admits. "But how can you argue? It's George Allen, he was an idol of mine."

The criticism from the press was so pointed that Allen felt he had to respond. He told the *Atlanta Constitution*, "This job will be like crossing the ocean in a canoe...but if it had been an easy job, I wouldn't have taken it." He told the *Philadelphia Daily News*, "The more impossible everyone said it was, the more I wanted to try it."

The rest of the campus responded as though Elvis had landed. With a sweep of his hand, Allen decided that the school's colors of brown and gold were ugly and requested they be changed to black and gold. "People were

The arrival of George Allen changed everything at the university, and quickly. *Courtesy Long Beach State.*

Allen with Ronald Reagan, just one example of his star power. *Courtesy Long Beach State.*

scared of him on campus," said Brady. "He came in and said, 'Bah, I don't like brown, it's black now.' And he just switched it!" Waving aside forty years of tradition like a nuisance, Allen's command was granted (the colors are black and gold to this day).

Just a few years prior, it had looked like football might be lost to the university. But suddenly, it had a legendary coach in his first college job since coaching Whittier College in 1956. Allen was such a big name that the city threw a big welcoming party for him. And Allen reached into his personal Rolodex and invited old friends like Frank Sinatra and President Reagan.

The cover of the media guide that year has a photo of Allen, accompanied by the words, "The Future is Now." It was a phrase he came up with while coaching the Redskins, a philosophy meant to explain why he believed in

Allen's 1990 team, the only team he was to coach at LBSU. *Courtesy Long Beach State.*

signing proven veteran players, as opposed to gambling on the draft and player development. It didn't help a team win a game that weekend in thinking how good a player could be in four or five years. That philosophy didn't necessarily fit at Long Beach, where the only thing one could talk about was potential.

The team lost its first game with Allen, 59–0, to Clemson. Then it lost, 27–13, to Utah State, followed by a 38–20 loss to San Diego State. "We have to get better players," Allen told *Sports Illustrated.* Of course, in the NCAA, that wasn't going to happen mid-season. So the team kept working. And it started winning. Players like Mark Seay helped lead a downright Allen-esque turnaround. The 49ers beat Pacific, Boise State and New Mexico State. After two losses, they won a pair, defeating Fullerton and Northridge and putting the team's record at 5–5 going into the 49ers last game, a home game against UNLV.

It was a chilly night at Vets, as always, when the team took the field against the Runnin' Rebels. Virtually nothing was at stake except the team's right to

With Allen came the crowds, but they quickly dried up after his death. *Courtesy Long Beach State.*

say it had a winning season at 6–5 instead of 5–6. For Allen, the outcome would decide his ability to keep his streak of winning records going. The 49ers fought hard that night, and they won, 29–20. Somebody dumped a bucket of ice water on Allen. The future was looking bright: the team would return a lot of players the next year, interest was growing and Allen had another two years on his contract. But within two months of the mid-November game, Allen would be dead. And the program wouldn't survive for long without him.

What Killed George Allen?

Anyone who has walked the sidelines of Vets Stadium in mid-November knows that it's not exactly the best place to take an ice bath, especially for a seventy-two-year-old. But Allen's team was excited, and it had helped him deliver his promise of the team's first winning season in five years. In celebration, some players dumped a Gatorade cooler filled with ice water on him. Allen would wryly remark later that the school couldn't afford Gatorade.

"I didn't see who poured it," said Brady, "And I don't think any of those people would admit they did it, because of the belief that it impacted his death. But we saw him wet afterwards, I know it happened."

Allen made a comment to a newspaper a few weeks before his death that he hadn't felt right since the ice bath. Keith Olbermann, the CBS sports reporter in Southern California at the time, was the first to take that comment and run with it, saying on a TV broadcast that Allen had died of pneumonia caused by the icy celebration. The legend was picked up and carried to every corner of the city and the country. Allen's death certificate, however, says that he died of a heart attack, not pneumonia (and besides, cold weather doesn't *actually* give you pneumonia).

Bill Brady saw Allen doing his usual rigorous prepractice run nine days before his death and said the coach looked totally healthy during his usual strenuous exercises. The *Los Angeles Times*, during the researching of this book, actually ran an article debunking the urban legend. In part, it reads:

> *George Allen did not die from pneumonia. Allen died from ventricular fibrillation, a variation of a cardiac arrest. Allen had a heart arrhythmia (an irregular heartbeat) and in late December 1990, Allen's heart began to quiver rather than contract properly. This led to his death. This was not caused by a Gatorade shower received more than a month earlier.*

Allen's son, George Allen Jr., told the *New York Times*, "He got a cold from it, but that was not the cause of his death. He had a heart arrhythmia. It had nothing to do with the Gatorade shower."

But while that might alleviate the consciences of a few over-eager players that night, Allen's death presented serious challenges to the university. Its star power was gone and, with him, any chance at an on-campus stadium or a major fundraising push. The school memorialized Allen by naming the multipurpose sports field after him, the only facility on campus named after a former athlete or coach. In the media file at the school, the Allen folder is still twice as thick as any of the Olympic or pro stars the school has produced. At the field dedication, the official athletic department speech put it best: "From the moment he stepped onto the Long Beach State campus, things changed."

Allen, for his part, appreciated the school. In a *Sports Illustrated* article written just four weeks before his death, he referred to it as his "most gratifying year" of coaching. But Allen knew as well as anyone else how much his personality meant to the team's future. And without him, the future wasn't *now* anymore—it was *then*.

A Program Disappears

Willie Brown took over as head coach in 1991, having served under Allen as an assistant. The attempt to link the program to its recent glory was obvious. "Coach Brown has incorporated many of Coach Allen's ideas into his personal football philosophy," reads a media guide from that year. It proudly proclaims, "The 1991 season looks bright." But bright it was not. The team had the same roster Allen motivated to a 6–5 finish, and the 49ers went 2–9, playing before a Vets audience where most of the fans came dressed as empty seats.

The program was shut down after the 1991 season, with a final record of 199–183–4. The 49ers' last win was against Utah State, 7–6, and their final game was a 37–36 loss to Fullerton. Since 1991, several attempts have been made by students or other organizations to bring the team back, but it's never been anywhere close to a financial possibility. Those who were around point to the team's dismal attendance in the latter (non–George Allen) years as a major obstacle and, because of Title IX, the school would have to add as many women's scholarships as it added football scholarships if it were to start a program again.

Guys like Brady are left to wonder what might have been had Allen not died, had the stadium been built, had the 49ers kept playing. "They wouldn't have dropped it," said Brady, shaking his head. "He had a multiyear vision of how he was going to change the program, and he'd started. They had architectural designs for the on-campus stadium. Think about how different things would be then. No, they wouldn't have dropped it. There's no way."

Other former players, like Severson, still resent that the administration once again asked for money from the community and still shut the team down despite purportedly raising a large amount of cash. "It's just a travesty not to have football," he said. "Everyone who played football there felt a

FUTURE FORTY-NINER SCHEDULES (All future schedules are tentative)					
1992		1993		1994	
Sept. 5	at Wyoming	Sept. 4	at Hawaii	Sept. 3	at Akron
Sept. 12	at UCLA	Sept. 11	at LSU	Sept. 10	at Oregon State
Sept. 26	at Oregon	Sept. 18	at San Diego St.	**SEPT. 17**	**BOISE STATE**
Oct. 3	at Hawaii	Sept. 25	at Utah	Oct. 1	at Pacific
Oct. 10	at San Jose St.	Oct. 2	at New Mexico St.	**OCT. 15**	**N. MEXICO ST.**
OCT. 17	**FRESNO ST.**	Oct. 9	at Arizona	Oct. 22	at San Jose St.
OCT. 24	**UNLV**	**OCT. 16**	**SAN JOSE ST.**	**OCT. 29**	**FRESNO ST.**
Oct. 31	at Utah State	Oct. 23	at Fresno St.	**NOV. 5**	**UNLV**
Nov. 7	at Pacific	Oct. 30	at UNLV	Nov. 12	at Utah St.
NOV. 14	**N. MEXICO ST.**	**NOV. 6**	**UTAH ST.**	**NOV. 19**	**CS FULLERTON**
NOV. 21	**CS FULLERTON**	**NOV. 20**	**PACIFIC**	(One game is to be added)	
		Nov. 27	at CS Fullerton		

The schedule that was never to be. Games that were meant to be played in 1992 were ultimately cancelled when the 49ers' program was dropped. *Courtesy Long Beach State.*

little betrayed. They were going to pull the plug anyway...they used us for donations for other programs. It's been a bitter pill to swallow."

When asked about the possibility of a team ever coming back, Severson laughed. "If [LBSU alum] Steven Spielberg endows it with about $25 million, or if I hit an oil field next week, maybe." Until that time, 49er fans of old will have their memories, and current students will have their "Undefeated Since 1991" shirts, supporting the school's most popular team, which just so happens to not exist anymore.

CHAPTER ELEVEN

Jim Stangeland

The Colonel

There's not really any argument in Long Beach against the fact that Jim Stangeland is the best college coach the city ever had. He is a member of the Long Beach City College, Long Beach State and Century Club Halls of Fame, and he coached three of the Vikings' five national championships, as well as two of the 49ers' three conference champion teams, including the only one in team history to make a bowl game appearance.

What you won't get from reading a history of the schools, however, is a full sense of Stangeland's influence on the city's football history. The Downey state champion track athlete and World War II bomber pilot put down roots in the city with his wife, and they raised their three daughters in Long Beach. Even after he left his Long Beach State job in 1974, he remained an active part of the city for several decades.

In 1957, Stangeland was one of the founding members of the Long Beach Century Club. Forty years later, even though he was two decades removed from his retirement from coaching, he was still making weekly phone calls to Larry Reisbig during Reisbig's tenure at LBCC. "I really respected him," said Reisbig, the only other man besides Stangeland to be the head coach at both of Long Beach's colleges. "He was not reluctant to give you his thoughts, either. We had some nice friendly arguments on Sundays after games. But it makes you think and evaluate what you're doing."

Stangeland was even more intimately involved in the coaching at a school he didn't even attend. When Dave Levy remembered taking over his alma mater Long Beach Poly in the late 1950s, he said that he and backfield coach

Bill Mulligan inherited a Wing-T offense. When they saw their running backs for the next year, the blindingly fast duo of Dee Andrews and Willie Brown, both coaches realized they needed a new offense. So the two of them went to Stangeland's house with a voice recorder the size of a suitcase. "We said, 'Jim, we've got speed, what can you do?' And he pulled out film of the Tight T that Pappy Waldorf had made popular at Cal, and we put that together in a few hours. Then we went and got some flashy uniforms, and the rest is history."

When Stangeland retired, he had won 81 percent of the football games he had coached. Although he was ninety years old at the time he was interviewed for this book, he still remembered specific play calls that led to those wins, and he said his coaching success came not from his strong sense of discipline (which earned him the nickname "The Colonel"), but from his attention to detail. And even at his age, Stangeland still speaks as a man enthralled with the sport:

> *I was a detailed coach—I coached every aspect of the game. Kickoff, kickoff returns, defense, offense...I went to clinics all over the United States and I took notes, and I talked to great coaches and I tried to put it all together. Because football is a game of vast variety, and it's terrible to neglect even one part of it—and if you do, that's the area you're going to get bombed in.*

Many times, men of Stangeland's age are said to have outlived their friends. But because of a true affection for his players and a lifetime of success, there is a steady stream of ex-players and assistants that travel to Huntington Beach to visit him. That's a testament to the impact he made not just on the field but outside the sidelines as well.

"Those were good years in Long Beach," he recalled, his sharp blue eyes gazing into the distance. "We kicked the ass of everyone else in the country." In doing so, Stangeland helped put Long Beach on the map.

CHAPTER TWELVE

LAKEWOOD

Everybody's Rival

Every good story needs a villain and, for almost every Long Beach football team, at one point or another, that villain has been the Lakewood Lancers.

Lakewood, the city, was founded in 1954 as a planned post–World War II community. It's essentially a suburb of Long Beach, running along the city's northern border. Lakewood doesn't have its own school system, and a dozen Long Beach Unified School District schools (LBUSD) help educate Lakewood youth. Lakewood High is one of those schools, and due to its LBUSD affiliation and proximity, the Lancers' football team, which began competing in 1957, has only ever belonged to the Harry J. Moore League, with the other Long Beach schools.

But from the start, schools like Poly, Wilson, Millikan and Jordan have seen Lakewood as the "other" in their group. The Lancers were suburban, while Long Beach's schools became increasingly urban. One of Lakewood's fiercest rivalries over the years has been with Millikan, a rivalry that makes sense, given the schools' strange shared history.

If there's such a thing as proximity infatuation, the Lakewood Lancers and Millikan Rams have long suffered from proximity revulsion. Less than three miles stand between the two campuses and, architecturally speaking, not much else separates them. To save money, LBUSD used the same blueprint to build the schools, which opened just one year apart (Millikan took its first students in 1956), both surfing the crest of the baby boom. The only difference between the campuses is the schools' colors, Lakewood's red clashing with Millikan's blue.

Like all good local rivalries, the Lancers and Rams got involved with a trophy, the only one still awarded for a rivalry series still within the Moore League: the Hamilton Trophy, named after a vice-principal who served at both schools and who was killed in a car accident. The winner of their annual meeting has the right to display the Hamilton and, in the last few years, it has been at Lakewood. For a time, though, that wasn't the case. Millikan went 6–0–1 in its first seven games against the Lancers, but then Lakewood hired John T. Ford as its coach in 1963.

The hard-nosed disciplinarian set about molding Lakewood's big linemen into disciplined blocking machines and succeeded. Lakewood has won eight Moore League titles, second only to Poly. Ford was the head coach of four of those teams during his reign from 1963–78. He also reversed the trend with Millikan, capturing the Hamilton ten of the eighteen times the teams met during his tenure.

Dave Radford, a member of Millikan's first-ever team and a former head coach of the Rams, said, "The competition there was terrific. The coaches were actually great friends, and so that competition was very high." The familiarity only increased in the late 1970s, when the teams were temporarily prevented from practicing at their campus fields because of a budget issue. Instead, the Rams and Lancers spent a few summers going against each other every day at El Dorado Park. "There were no secrets," said Radford.

In addition to getting them on the right track against their rivals, Ford also coached the only Lakewood team to make it to the finals. In 1970, in a game between two Lancers teams, Lakewood and Bishop Amat, the teams battled to a 17–17 draw before a crowd of 31,012 at the Los Angeles Coliseum, the fourth-biggest attendance in CIF postseason history. At the time, ties were (heartbreakingly) determined by who had more possession across the fifty-yard line, giving Bishop Amat an 18–17 decision in the record books. That would be the end of Lakewood's postseason success for quite some time. They got one win before being eliminated in 1972, 1982 and 1983, but wouldn't return to the semifinals until 2004.

The arrival of Thadd MacNeal before the 2006 season put Lakewood back in the mix and helped spark the Moore League's premier recent rivalry between the Lancers and Poly. MacNeal went 45–15 in his five years as coach of the Lancers, installing them as the top contender against the Jackrabbits. He was 25–5 in the Moore League, with four of those losses coming to Poly. More important to the rabid Lakewood following, one of those wins was against the Jackrabbits, too. MacNeal's Lancers were the ones, in 2009, to end Poly's state-record league winning streak at eighty games. It was the first time Lakewood had beaten Poly in twenty-six years.

While it's perhaps the similarities between them that powered Millikan's dislike of Lakewood, the rivalry between Poly and Lakewood was highlighted by their differences. Their meetings from 2007 on have all drawn at least ten thousand fans in a rivalry series dubbed the Moore League Super Bowl. Many of those fans were there to root on not just the teams but whole societal visions. Poly, in the heart of Long Beach, was the multiracial representation of a multiracial city, where no one race holds a majority. Lakewood was the name-bearing standard of a team where the Caucasian population is 22 percent larger than any other racial group.

That streak of racial isolationism has highlighted Lakewood's clash with many teams. Part of the city's population boom came as a result of white flight from an increasingly urbanizing Long Beach in the early 1960s. The city's motto, "Times change, values don't," hearkens back to a post–World War II era that Long Beach has left behind. Indeed, stepping onto Lakewood's campus field, named after Ford, often feels like stepping back in time.

Across from the grandstands, fans park their RVs on the street and sit on the roofs, watching the game over the chain-link fence that separates the school's field from the neighborhood around it. The small-town team stepped into the big time in 2008 and 2009, when MacNeal took them to back-to-back CIF semifinals for the first time since Ford had done it in 1969 and 1970. Further heightening their rivalry was a meeting between the Lancers and Poly in the semis in 2008, a game Poly would win en route to its eighteenth CIF title.

Lakewood fans have never been short on passion, and the Moore League is certainly a more entertaining place when the Lancers are competing with the top-tier teams. After all, there's nothing more exciting than a rivalry game. And whether it was Millikan in the schools' early years, Poly more recently or any other team in the league that you could name, everyone has had a rivalry with Lakewood; it's the team everyone else loves to hate.

CHAPTER THIRTEEN

Long Beach Jordan

The Bad Luck Panthers

Jordan High opened after the Long Beach earthquake of 1933. For three years, classes were actually held in the North Long Beach YMCA building and in the Houghton Park recreation center. But as Long Beach's population continued to grow, so too did the need for new schools, and construction began on a lot next to the park. Jordan would soon open its doors at its permanent location, at 6500 Atlantic Avenue, six miles up the road from Long Beach's first high school.

By 1935, sports were already a way of life, and teams began organizing on the undeveloped fields before they even had a name. Football, of course, would lead the way forward. Students were initially known as pioneers, since North Long Beach at that time was thought of as the city's undeveloped frontier. The name trailblazers was also under consideration for the same reasons.

But out of the wilds of North Long Beach and the marshland around the river came an answer. While the football team was practicing, players noticed that a midnight-black kitten had been sitting on the sidelines, watching them practice. The next day, it returned. And the day after that, and the day after that. In John Dixon's history of Long Beach sports, he said that Jordan's first football coach, Dick Cline, commented, "One of the players said that it looked like a panther."

It was certainly a more imposing nickname than the Kittens, and it stuck. Every team at the school quickly adopted the name, and the Panthers of North Long Beach were born. One of the old names stuck around, however, as the school's yearbook is still titled "The Trailblazer."

The school's early years comprised some of the best moments in Jordan's history. There was a host of great Panthers in the 1940s and '50s, but since the founding of the Moore League in 1957, the football world has spun away from Jordan.

The only three Moore League titles Jordan has been able to claim were in 1988, 1990 and 1994—and all three of them were tied with Poly (the '94 championship was tied with Lakewood as well, in a bizarre three-way title). Coach Scott Meyer led a brief revival late in the first decade of the 2000s. His quarterback and starting safety, John Timu, was the Moore League Player of the Year as a junior in 2008, a year that the Moore League was so strong Poly and Lakewood met in the CIF semifinals. Jordan lost to Mater Dei in the first round that year but, with Timu and a few other Division 1 players back for 2009, big things were expected of the Panthers.

Until, that is, the luck of the black cat came crashing down on them. Timu was scrambling in the open field in a game early that season and, at one point when he planted his foot, he felt his knee go sideways. He had torn several ligaments. Timu was out for the season, meaning the team's best offensive and defensive player, as well as its only punter and kicker, wouldn't be available. For the rest of the season, sixteen of the twenty-two starters on opening night would go down for at least one game with an injury. It was a dark season for a team that had been so optimistic, and while Panthers fans have enjoyed watching Timu and Jordan teammate Princeton Fuimaono competing at the University of Washington, they would certainly love to see the Panthers competing again within city limits.

Several decades ago, that would never have been a question. In 1940, quarterback Glenn Shoop won CIF State championships in the long jump and the low hurdles and won All-CIF honors as the signal caller for the football team. He guided Jordan to the playoffs that year, where it lost to Santa Barbara, the eventual CIF champions. Shoop was named All-American that year.

In 1947, the team defeated Poly 7–6 and Wilson 27–12, the first time it had beaten the city's other two high schools in the same season. Bud Woodward was the driving force on the offense, winning CIF Player of the Year for his one-man offensive show. Woodward, whom former *Press-Telegram* sports editor John Dixon described as being "constructed like an NFL lineman," gained 1,149 yards on the ground and rushed for 14 touchdowns. He also threw passes for an additional half-dozen scores and scored 133 of the team's 153 points that year. He took the Panthers to the CIF quarterfinals, where they lost to Alhambra. Two years later, the

Jordan quarterback Glenn Shoop, an All-American in his senior year in 1940. *Courtesy* Press-Telegram.

Panthers had another All-American in George Timberlake, a fullback who was an All-American on LBCC's 1950 national championship team and who later played at USC.

Pride in the Panther tradition at this point was high enough that the students started a war bond drive that was so successful that they actually got a B-17 bomber named after the school. The Jordan Panther, as it was called, would see action in the Pacific Theatre of World War II.

The year 1950 saw an athlete who may have been the greatest t ever to come out of Jordan. Bob Davenport was a star fullback who broke most of the school's rushing records and who would go on to great heights at UCLA, lettering three years and scoring the first touchdown in the 1954 Rose Bowl against Michigan State. He was named the Bruins' most valuable player in 1955 and was an All-American his junior and senior seasons, scoring eighteen touchdowns despite serving primarily as a blocking fullback. Davenport was also a founding member of the Campus Crusade for Christ organization at UCLA, a group that has grown to be active on over two thousand campuses around the world.

In 1988, the Panthers won their first Moore League title, thanks to running back Johnny Robinson, who gained 1,463 yards and scored fourteen touchdowns that year, earning Moore League and City Player of the Year honors by helping to make history.

Over time, however, things began to deteriorate at the school. Alumni support disappeared, and money grew scarce. One positive is that Pacific Islander players like Timu, Fuimaono and Tani Maka have become the new face of the school's football program, thanks to the large Polynesian population in North Long Beach. Also, in 1995, the school made history when Lorenza Coronado caught a two-yard touchdown pass in a 31–14 win over St. Bernard, the first time a girl had scored a touchdown in a high school football game in California.

But for the most part, the story at Jordan has been one more typical of an inner-city school struggling to maintain a sense of identity. In 1992, assistant coach Ondra Guidry, a Jordan grad class of 1985, was shot and killed at a fraternity party in Las Vegas. In 2003, in a noncontact passing league game against Moore League newbie Cabrillo, the Panthers and Jaguars players got into a brawl, which led to the firing of then-head coach Willie Guillory. Following the 2009 season, head coach Scott Meyer departed North Town for Long Beach Wilson, where he was a third-generation player, to coach his son, a fourth-generation Bruin—the exact kind of link to a history and tradition that the Panthers have been searching for.

Jordan's fullback Bob Davenport, who went on to All-American honors at UCLA in 1954 and 1955. *Courtesy* Press-Telegram.

It's a process. At the time of this writing, a Facebook group established for the Panthers' Booster Club had just sixty-one members. Keep in mind that this is a school with eighty years of history to its name and a list of graduates that includes All-Americans and current Division 1 athletes. The team hasn't received nearly as much support from its community as it deserves.

But hope springs eternal at Jordan. As of last year, it has a new principal, Shawn Ashley, who presided over Long Beach Poly for more than a decade of its recent glory years. There is even more optimism surrounding scheduled renovations, which are estimated to cost around $105 million. Those improvements, which will include completely revamping the athletic fields, are scheduled to be completed in 2015.

With new leadership and an ability to compete in the growing high school facilities arms race, things could be looking up for the Panthers as these black cats try to shed their shoddy luck.

CHAPTER FOURTEEN

THE MILK BOWL

Long-Lost Tradition

So much of what makes Long Beach football great is the sport's interaction with its traditions. Sadly, when combing through old newspapers, you are sometimes reminded of great traditions that are, well, lost to history. Chief among these, without question, is the old Milk Bowl game.

In 1948, two men came up with the idea to convert Long Beach citizens' love for their football teams into money for other school programs. The first was Harry J. Moore, former Poly vice-principal and Wilson principal, who was then an assistant superintendent with the LBUSD; of course, he would go on to lasting fame in Long Beach when the city named its sports league after him. The second was Douglas Newcomb, then the superintendent of the LBUSD, who would also achieve a lasting legacy when one of the city's schools, the Newcomb Academy, was named after him.

The idea both men had was to have all of the city's public schools scrimmage against each other. Tickets were sold on all of the city's campuses, and for the first two years, the game, which featured Poly, Wilson and Jordan, was played on the last day of the season. The game was quickly dubbed the Milk Bowl, since it benefited the PTA's Milk Fund, providing students with something healthy to drink.

Over time, the game evolved. After the first two years, it was played the first week of the year, instead of the last. In 1953, it was moved to Vets Stadium (previously, it had been rotating from campus to campus) and, later that decade, Millikan and Lakewood were added.

The event was wildly successful as a fundraiser and a point of civic pride. Over 5,000 came out for the first game in 1948, and that quickly grew. In 1970, it hit an all-time high with a record attendance of 18,391 Long Beach football fans. The events were not just fun displays of football but full-on pageants, with the bands and cheerleaders from each team performing, occasionally doing special Milk Bowl routines (in 1948, Jordan's band formed into the shape of a milk bottle and played Farmer in the Dell).

The crowds grew so great that director Irwin Allen brought his camera to Vets to use its crowd in a scene in his 1977 feature film, *Viva Knievel.* Along with the fun, there was some danger. Poly running back and star-to-be Harvey Crow blew his knee out on the first play of the 1960 game.

Alas, not all great traditions are built to last, and by the late 1980s, fan interest was waning. After fewer than a thousand fans showed up for the 1989 game, the district decided to cancel the annual event. Every few years, someone brings up the idea of resurrecting it, but no one has been able to make a push forward. So for now, this piece of history remains just that.

Thanks to the *Press-Telegram*'s Billy Witz and Tim Grobaty for their excellent histories of the Milk Bowl.

CHAPTER FIFTEEN

LONG BEACH MILLIKAN

The Rams and Their Rings

Millikan has also struggled to compete in recent years, but for one brief, shining period, it stood with the best teams in Southern California. Millikan was founded in the suburbs of East Long Beach in 1956, part of the post–World War II baby boom, which saw the LBUSD scrambling to come up with new schools to tutor thousands of additional students.

There is no great story behind Millikan's mascot, unless you're a big fan of wordplay. The school is named for Robert A. Millikan, whose initials spell "RAM." The Rams have claimed four Moore League football titles, winning one by themselves in 1973, tying with Compton in 1977 and 1979 and tying with Poly in 1985. But what sets Millikan apart from Lakewood, Jordan, Wilson and Cabrillo, is that the Rams won a pair of CIF titles in 1977 and '79.

The success came virtually out of nowhere. Millikan had fielded great players in the past but never great teams. Gary Garrison starred in the early 1960s as an end-backer and a flanker, committing full time to wide receiver at San Diego State (where he still holds most of the school's career receiving records, including 26 career touchdowns) and then graduating to 12 years of pro football. He was drafted by the Eagles in the sixth round in 1965 and was then traded to the Chargers. Garrison, nicknamed "The Ghost" because tacklers often couldn't find him, spent 11 years with the Chargers, notching 7,500 yards and 58 touchdowns. He was named to 4 pro bowls and is a member of the San Diego State and Chargers Halls of Fame.

Gary Garrison, who went from Millikan to San Diego State to the Chargers. *Courtesy* Press-Telegram.

But none of the teams Garrison played on in Ram Town would come close to grabbing playoff glory. In fact, prior to 1977, the Rams had never won a postseason game, making their run to the CIF Coastal Championship that much more remarkable, as they went a perfect 4–0 that postseason under head coach Dick DeHaven, who coached both Millikan championship teams.

The Rams' first playoff win was over Muir, 15–6, and then they sent off West Torrance, 25–14. The next week, in the semifinal, they faced Long Beach Poly at Vets and defeated the Jackrabbits 27–7 in a game that could have been seen as flipping the course of the city's football future. The next week, they would defeat Arcadia 34–14 in the championship game, forever changing the program. From that day forward, even if they lost all their games, the Rams would be "CIF Champs." In that game, Millikan went up 19–0 and was able to fend off a feisty Arcadia team late in the game. The Rams were known for a relentless, long-driving offense, which wore down the Apaches throughout the evening.

"We came out and played the way we've played all year," tackle Randy Hausauer told the *Arcadia Tribune*. "It was a team effort."

But given the Rams' previous lack of success, nobody could have imagined it. In fact, the team's defensive coordinator had actually scheduled a Hawaii vacation for the weekend of the championship game, a pretty telling example of expectations for the Rams at that time.

Two years later, they tied for the 1979 Moore League title with the Compton Tarbabes, clinching a share of the title with a 35–0 win over Poly in the last game of the year. The Tarbabes had beaten them 21–20 during the regular season, after head coach Dick DeHaven decided to go for two. The situation presented itself once again in the championship game, where the Rams once again faced Compton, this time at Anaheim Stadium for the CIF Coastal Division championship.

The teams went into overtime after tying at 14, and Compton scored a touchdown on its first play. Millikan battled and managed to score, but the coaches knew the Rams couldn't win a sustained fight with the Tarbabes. DeHaven looked at coach Dave Radford, a member of his defensive staff. Radford put two fingers against his chest. "I gave him a look like, 'This is as close as we're going to get,'" recalled Radford. "I just did not see us keeping them out of the end zone. So he called 44 Bear, and we handed off to Frank Baker, and he goes in for two." Millikan won, 22–21, on the ballsiest play call in Moore League history that concluded the league's most historically significant game, the only time two of its members played each other for a CIF title.

"It was a huge advantage that we knew our opponents in those games," said DeHaven. "Everything fell into place those years." Those teams were known for incredible technique and skill. Radford said DeHaven only ever used between three and five plays on offense per game, but the Rams executed them so well they couldn't be stopped.

The Rams' flame burned brightly, but quickly, too. The next year, the team went to the quarterfinals before bowing out. In that four-year span, it won ten playoff games. In the fifty-two years around that stretch, it only won one other postseason game, defeating only one team in 1986. But losing its postseason mojo didn't mean that the Rams didn't have other peaks in their history. Millikan alums often recall two games, one in 1985 and another in 2009, as the Rams' last pair of wins over Poly.

The 1985 game is still such a sore subject for Jerry Jaso, the Poly coach at the time, that he said he would rather not speak about it in an interview. The Jackrabbits went on to win a CIF title that year, but the Rams got a share of the Moore League title, thanks to an improbable comeback. Millikan led 9–0, only to see the Jackrabbits sprint ahead 13–9 with fifty-nine seconds left. The Rams fumbled the ball away, and the Poly players began celebrating, something several Rams fans in the stands still remember vividly.

But Poly quarterback Mike Herring threw a pass, and Millikan's Bob Brown created an indelible moment by picking the pass off, setting up quarterback Cliff Mosley's touchdown pass to Ed Robinson with five seconds left, giving Millikan a 15–13 victory.

"I wouldn't want to talk about that game if I were Jerry either," Radford said with a smile. By that time, Radford had moved up from assistant to head coach of the Rams, an appointment that must have seemed like the emergence of King Arthur to Millikan fans. Radford had played for the first Millikan team ever, was a member of the school's first graduating class and, in fact, was the school's first student body president. But he had also compiled an extensive coaching resume. By the time he retired, Radford coached at six of Long Beach's high schools and colleges. That included a long stint at Poly, which informed the way he coached his teams against the Jackrabbits.

"Too many teams give them that mystique," he said. "I looked at them as the kids I had sitting in my class. They're just normal kids. They're as screwed up as our kids, so we never let our guys see them as monsters."

It was a win that would see itself mirrored twenty-five years later, and the 1985 team was in attendance, commemorated as the last Rams team to beat Poly. In 2009, Millikan's Alden Darby led a group of Rams that didn't belong on the same field as the Jackrabbits, at least on paper. "What'd they have, nine or ten Division 1 guys? And we had one," recalled former coach Kirk Diego. "Yeah, that was stupid." The Jackrabbits outweighed the Rams by twenty-five pounds (on average) per lineman, and were faster and

Coach Dave Radford, who took Millikan to a Moore League title in 1985. Radford was the school's first-ever student body president and a member of Millikan's first graduating class. *Courtesy* Press-Telegram.

stronger. But Millikan had a rare leader in Darby, a Poly-area kid who took a bus across town to play for the Rams, eventually becoming a highly sought-after recruit who went on to play at Arizona State.

Darby was playing on basically one leg at that point because of an injury, but he put his team on his back on both sides of the ball. As a quarterback, he threw three touchdowns, putting his team up 21–14 after three quarters. But Poly, despite five interceptions and a number of other mistakes, rallied back to tie the game with 1:07 remaining, sending the game into overtime with the score knotted at 28–28.

The game had progressed slowly, thanks to 250 yards in penalties and ten turnovers between the teams, so most of the other football games in the city were done. As the teams lined up for overtime, word had spread across the city, and people were pouring in from other games. Stands that had been half full at the start of the game were suddenly packed to bursting. Fans were double-parked on Palo Verde Avenue, standing on top of their cars to see how the game ended, indifferent to getting a ticket. Families who lived in the houses across the street grabbed their kids and hurried over to see how the game would play out, as did almost all of the Moore League's other coaches.

Millikan would score first, on a touchdown strike from Darby to Silver Vaifanua; Poly would answer on a one-yard touchdown run. The Jackrabbits elected to go for two. A deflected pass meant they didn't get it, and the Rams could start celebrating like it was 1985 again. Fans came down out of the stands, the team ran all over the field, the coaches threw their headsets up in the air. On Palo Verde, fans were jumping up and down on top of their cars. Lakewood's and Wilson's coaches were among the first to congratulate Diego in person.

"That is a highlight that, well, I'll never forget," Diego said. "And neither will any of those Millikan kids." And nobody will forget the performance of Darby, who threw three touchdowns, ran another one in and, on defense, picked off a pass and made four tackles.

"That's probably the best football game I've covered in Long Beach," said the *Press-Telegram*'s Bob Keisser, who's been covering games since 1990. "It was like Poly was star-crossed. The Rams were so totally spent by the middle of the fourth quarter you just couldn't see how they were going to hang on. It was Darby and a couple of the guys on defense who pulled themselves back off the ground and made the plays to win that game."

While other schools have struggled with discipline and organizational issues, the problems facing Millikan have always been much simpler. And nobody knew it better than Diego, who guided the team to a third-place finish in 2002, its best mark of the decade.

"I don't know what it is in the water, but for the most part we are so much smaller and slower than everyone else in the league. It's amazing. We just grow 'em a little different on this side of town. And the players we get historically that were good football players were overflow from Poly, or Jordan, or they were from those areas but chose us."

The frustration in East Long Beach has been palpable. After consecutive 1–9 seasons, Diego was removed from his post following the 2011 season. A well-respected developer of young men and a high-character guy, Diego said at the time that he perhaps didn't fit the mold of the win-first modern high school football ethos.

Athletic director Chris Kinder is hopeful things will turn around for the Rams. "A lot of times it's not so much about winning and losing as it is about competing," he said. "We need to get back to that. I'm not saying we're going to be division champions or anything like that, but we need to be able to get back to a competitive level. That's the road we're on right now."

CHAPTER SIXTEEN

CABRILLO

The Jaguars' New Spots

It is never easy being the little brother, but imagine if the oldest of your six big brothers had over a 100 years of experience and history on you. Long Beach football, as you know by now, is a world of rich traditions: championships, big moments, players going on to success at the next level. Even the schools that have lost touch with their glory years can at least point back to that distant past. Not so for the Cabrillo Jaguars.

Cabrillo was built in 1995, exactly 100 years after Long Beach's first high school opened. In the last decade and a half, its enrollment numbers have exceeded 4,000, putting the school on par with the other members of the LBUSD and the Moore League, at least in terms of enrollment. In terms of athletic competition, not so much. Since its inception and since joining the Moore League, Cabrillo has won just one title—not one football title, one Moore League title. Period. Across all sports. And it was in fútbol, not football.

Darin Parson originated the program as the Jaguars' first football coach when they began play in 1998. Parson guided them to a 5–5 record that year, when Cabrillo competed independently. The Jaguars spent the next four years in the lowly Suburban League before moving up to the Moore League in 2003. Parson motivated his team to a 4–2 mark in the Moore League that year and the Jaguars' first-ever playoff berth.

Since then, the Jaguars have struggled, trying on new coaches every couple of years and not finding much success. They had a three-year no-win streak in the Moore League until 2010 and then, in 2011, they equaled their greatest Moore League success to date, tying for second place with a league record of 4–2. That bettered their league win total from the previous five years combined, which was just three.

The wonderful and terrible thing about high school football, or any sport, is that you never know where it's going. In the 1940s, nobody at Jordan would have been able to imagine the Panthers' disappointing lean decades ahead. In the 1960s, nobody at Millikan could have foreseen the Rams winning two CIF titles in three years. And likewise, nobody knows where Cabrillo will be in five years or even ten. The wonderful thing about a history of football in Long Beach is that it is always being written, season after season, Friday night after Friday night.

APPENDIX

Poly NFL Players

Entered NFL	Name	Main NFL Team	College
1927	Roy "Bullet" Baker	Green Bay	USC/ Santa Clara
1927	Jim Lawson	NY Yankees, LA Wildcats	Stanford
1929	Jack Evans	Green Bay	Cal
1929	Don Hill	Green Bay	Stanford
1931	Corrie Artman	NY Giants	Stanford
1935	Norm "Red" Franklin	Brooklyn	Oregon State
1939	Kelly Moan	Cleveland	West Virginia
1946	Quentin Klenk	Buffalo	USC
1949	Sam Cathcart	San Francisco	UCSB

Entered NFL	Name	Main NFL Team	College
1950	Royal Cathcart	San Francisco	UCSB
1951	Bill Jessup	San Francisco	USC
1958	Johnny Morris	Chicago	UCSB
1960	Henry Wallace	San Diego	Pacific
1962	Gerry McDougall	San Diego	UCLA
1964	Willie Brown	LA Rams	USC
1965	Mike Giers	NY Giants	USC
1966	Mike Kellogg	Denver	Santa Clara
1966	Jeff Smith	NY Giants	USC
1968	Earl McCullough	Detroit	USC
1969	Gene Washington	San Francisco	Stanford
1970	Carl Weathers	Oakland	San Diego State
1977	Tony Hill	Dallas	Stanford
1983	Stephone Paige	Kansas City	Fresno State
1983	James McDonald	LA Rams	USC
1983	Kendall Williams	Baltimore	Arizona State
1983	Andre Tyler	Tampa Bay	Stanford

Entered NFL	**Name**	**Main NFL Team**	**College**
1984	Randall Morris	Seattle	Tennessee
1985	David Howard	Minnesota	Oregon State/ LB State
1987	Charles Clinton	Houston	San Jose State
1987	Kirk Jones	Cleveland	UNLV
1987	Al Williams	San Diego	Nevada
1988	Dennis Price	NY Jets	UCLA
1988	Chuckie Miller	Indianapolis	UCLA
1990	Mark Carrier	Chicago	USC
1991	Leonard Russell	New England	Arizona State
1992	Marquez Pope	San Diego	Fresno State
1994	Willie McGinest	New England	USC
1994	James Burton	Chicago	Hawaii/ Fresno State
1995	Don Sasa	San Diego	Washington State
1997	Omar Stoutmire	NY Giants	Fresno State
1998	Brandon Whiting	Philadelphia	Cal
2001	Ken-Yon Rambo	Dallas	Ohio State

Entered NFL	Name	Main NFL Team	College
2002	Marques Anderson	Green Bay	UCLA
2003	Kareem Kelly	New Orleans	USC
2003	Mark Washington	San Francisco	ASU
2003	Darrell Rideaux	Indianapolis	USC
2004	Larry Croom	Arizona	UNLV
2004	Samie Parker	Kansas City	Oregon
2004	Chris Lewis	Arizona	Stanford
2005	Manuel Wright	Miami	USC
2006	Darnell Bing	Detroit	USC
2006	Winston Justice	Philadelphia	USC
2006	Marcedes Lewis	Jacksonville	UCLA
2006	Raymond Washington	Oakland	Fresno State
2007	Pago Togafau	Arizona	Idaho State
2008	DeSean Jackson	Philadelphia	Cal
2010	Donovan Warren	NY Jets	Michigan
2010	Terrence Austin	Washington	UCLA
2011	Jurrell Casey	Tennessee	USC

Entered NFL	**Name**	**Main NFL Team**	**College**
2011	Travon Patterson	San Diego	USC/Colorado
2011	Kenny Rowe	San Francisco	Oregon
2011	Derrick Jones	Oakland	USC/Oregon/ Cal/ U Penn
2011	Conan Amituanai	Minnesota	Arizona
2012	Tray Session	Oakland	Nevada

INDEX

G

H

I

J

K

L

R

S

About the Author

Mike Guardabascio was born and raised in Long Beach, California. He has been writing professionally for ten years and has been published in over two dozen magazines and newspapers. He has been covering high school and college sports in Long Beach for the last five years and is co-editor of the *Grunion Gazette* sports section and the popular website GazettesSports.com. He lives in Long Beach with his wife, Shar. He can be reached via email at mike@gazettes.com.